"Patler takes us to the racing heart of the Big Wav[e] by our side, pointing out profound lessons for entr[...]
—Sheila Heen, CEO, Triad Consulting, co-auth[or]
faculty, Harvard Law School

"The book makes me want to jump out of my business suite . . . grab a board, . . . and hit the waves!" —Les McCabe, president & CEO, Global Green USA

". . . exceptional book about surfing and business . . . a compelling read and a must for aspiring business professionals." —Anthony Vidergauz, CEO/founder, California Closets

"I learned a lot about entrepreneurs. I learned a lot about innovation. Most importantly, I learned what it takes to be really good at both."
—Allan Calarco, faculty member, Center for Creative Leadership

"Quite simply, the book inspired me! " —Jim Patrick, senior vice president, Wealth Management, Merrill Lynch

"*Make Your Own Waves* has now been added to our Day One onboarding as required reading to provide a roadmap for what it will take to be successful in our company. . . . A fantastic read." —Bill Akins, senior vice president, Business Innovation, Rockfish

"Packed with sage start-up advice from a guy who has seen it all . . ."
—Bernie Nagle, executive director, Precision Machined Parts Association

"Real, tangible, outcomes-based. It's the type of book that you want to keep pencil and paper near to take down notes."
—Fasie Malherbe, CEO, Lobster Ink

"Louis pulls together a masterful guide to innovation through the rigor of an accomplished researcher, the wisdom of a seasoned practitioner, and the art of a great storyteller." —Jeff Amerine, founding principal, Startup Junkie Consulting

"Undoubtedly Louis's work inspires and skills people to be wave riders whether the waves are in the ocean or in a changing world." —Peter Pattenden, managing director, Talent Mondial

". . . A thought provoking, research-rich business book based on his deceptively simple Surfers Rules . . ." —Holly Stiel, president, Thank You Very Much Inc.

"*Make Your Own Waves* takes you on an insightful and compelling journey, drawing parallels between the tenacious preparation of Big Wave surfers and the relentless perseverance of innovators and entrepreneurs."

—Dot van Hoorn, head of people, Lobster Ink

"Brilliantly insightful and compelling . . ."

—John Suttle, CEO, Suttle & Associates

"Louis Patler has written a great guide for the mindset and skillset that is required for entrepreneurs in these competitive yet opportune times."

—Michael Bennett, CIO (ret.), BAE Systems

"A unique guide to success in hazardous conditions through planning and preparation. Big wave experience is not required to appreciate this book!"
—Paul Tomita, Staniford Tomita LLP, mentor for the Telluride Venture Accelerator and the University of San Francisco Entrepreneurial Ventures Legal Services Project

"*Make Your Own Waves* offers powerful, inspiring and wise ideas . . . An easy yet rich read. I can take this book to the beach as well as the boardroom."

—Marilou McFarlane, CEO, Edufii, Inc., and mentor, SXSW Interactive

"For those considering starting a business this book is a fun and informative read. And maybe you will take up surfing too." —Marion McGovern, founder, M Squared Consulting

"An easy-to-digest guide to entrepreneurship and taking risks."

—Kristin Luna, journalist

"The Surfer's Rules . . . offers a clear path to success . . . exactly what every entrepreneur and innovator needs." —Parker Lee, co-author of *The Art of Opportunity*

LOUIS PATLER

MAKE YOUR OWN WAVES

The Surfer's Rules for Innovators
and Entrepreneurs

AMACOM

AMERICAN MANAGEMENT ASSOCIATION
New York • Atlanta • Brussels • Chicago • Mexico City • San Francisco
Shanghai • Tokyo • Toronto • Washington, D.C.

Bulk discounts available. For details visit:
www.amacombooks.org/go/specialsales
Or contact special sales: Phone: 800-250-5308 |
Email: specialsls@amanet.org
View all the AMACOM titles at: www.amacombooks.org
American Management Association: www.amanet.org

This publication is designed to provide accurate and authoritative information in regard to the subject matter covered. It is sold with the understanding that the publisher is not engaged in rendering legal, accounting, or other professional service. If legal advice or other expert assistance is required, the services of a competent professional person should be sought.

Names: Patler, Louis, author.
Title: Make your own waves : the surfer's rules for innovators and
    entrepreneurs / Louis Patler.
Description: New York, NY : AMACOM, [2016] | Includes bibliographical
    references and index.
Identifiers: LCCN 2016001363 (print) | LCCN 2016009670 (ebook) | ISBN
    9780814437230 (hardcover : alk. paper) | ISBN 9780814437247 (ebook)
Subjects: LCSH: Success in business. | Business planning. | Entrepreneurship.
Classification: LCC HF5386 .P346 2016 (print) | LCC HF5386 (ebook) | DDC
    658.4/21--dc23
LC record available at http://lccn.loc.gov/2016001363

ABOUT AMA

American Management Association (www.amanet.org) is a world leader in talent development, advancing the skills of individuals to drive business success. Our mission is to support the goals of individuals and organizations through a complete range of products and services, including classroom and virtual seminars, webcasts, webinars, podcasts, conferences, corporate and government solutions, business books, and research. AMA's approach to improving performance combines experiential learning—learning through doing—with opportunities for ongoing professional growth at every step of one's career journey.

To the waters, people and culture of
Hanalei, Kauai
For all you have given to me, my wife, my children
and now, my grandchildren.

&

In memory of and inspired by:
Mike Moser
Jay Moriarity
Brock Little

CONTENTS

CONTENTS

FOREWORD

SURFING, LIKE ENTREPRENEURSHIP, TAKES COURAGE.
I know this from spending two decades exploring the link
between the principles of surfing and business. I've written
about it in my books *The Surfer's Code* and *The Code*. I depicted
it in a film, *Bustin' Down the Door*, and I've lectured about it at
schools, universities and Fortune 500 companies. But I learned
about courage at Pipeline.

Phil Edwards, a surfing legend, rode the Banzai Pipeline for
the first time in the mid 1960s. Surfers had watched it for decades knowing the wave would punish any mistake with a vi-
cious wipeout or worse. Over the ensuing 50 years Pipeline has
become the benchmark of success, skill and courage—succeed
at Pipeline and a surfer carries that aura of confidence all over
the world. I was obsessed with Pipeline and as a 10-year-old, I
had a picture of it above my bed knowing that was where I
would be challenged to my core.

Particularly dangerous waves at a handful of breaks around the
world kill surfers each year. Mavericks has killed and Teahupo'o
too. However the Banzai Pipeline is a serial killer—it breaks 50
yards from the shore over a coral reef with dangerous riptides.

As a young boy, when surfing Pipeline the first few times, I would feel the fear rising as I got closer to that moment when one paddles over the edge, propelled forward by the wave's energy and the force of gravity. One has to make a quick decision and the worst moments come when you get stuck in the valley of indecision and the *wave* makes the decision, and metes out punishment for that failure to choose. Pipeline is all about totally committed decisions and I learned early that riding the wave successfully was an apt metaphor for any risky endeavor in life or business—take the drop with absolute commitment.

One day, soon after I had just won the World Surfing Championships, the youngest surfer ever to do so, I was riding a surfboard nicknamed the Pink Banana, a revolutionary and innovative piece of equipment with extreme curve (hence the name) that had enabled me to change my technique from one of stylish survival to powerful and radical maneuvering. I was young, strong and felt invincible.

I paddled out towards the second reef and the wave I wanted, swung around, and paddled hard with swift hand-over-hand strokes to match the wave's speed. The wave stood up vertically as it crested, enabling me to paddle over the edge of water, like descending a waterfall, using gravity to speed down the face. I jammed my turn at the ideal moment, thinking my mind and body were perfectly coordinated, while the wave started to throw out ahead of me.

As I dropped down the face of the wave I could see it was changing quickly as all the wave's power now approached the first reef, from the west and from the north. Imagine two waves coming towards each other and combining, exponentially increasing in force, speed and ferocity.

After my bottom turn I was now at maximum speed, experiencing the most intimate moment a surfer has with the ocean, riding deep inside the tube, in slow motion, like riding through dripping sculpted glass. I was 30 feet back inside the wave, invisible to anyone watching from shore, when the wave sped up, and so did I. Then, perhaps twenty feet in front of me, I noticed the water was a sinister black for a 15-yard stretch over shallow coral. I was in a high-risk situation, balanced on that razor between success and failure, with my only option being to do what had never been done. I had to innovate.

With my faith, my will, and my board I instinctively leaned forward into the danger, into the fear. My board accelerated, and behind me the wave heaved and exploded, blasting out a wild gasp of compressed air. I was shot forward, riding across the black coral at maximum velocity, then bursting out into the sunlight, over green water and soft sand, and into to my own internal anthem of valor and courage.

Louis Patler's book illustrates that surfing is a metaphor for how to face the black coral reefs of business and life. The rules one learns in the waves can be directly translated to the waves of business. He shows us that success in business is dependent on many tried and true factors that we surfers know well: preparation, focus, teamwork, innovation, mindfulness, commitment, perseverance, integrity, and what one doesn't hear much about, courage. His deep insight into some of the most courageous of all, the big wave surfers, shines a light on the importance of courage.

To be an innovator in business means to be cognizant of the risk and failure, but still go forward with strength and absolute commitment. To be courageous in the water and in the marketplace is not an absence of fear, but a keen awareness of it, and requires domination over it. By moving *towards* it, by making a deliberate decision to lean *into* it, you break down barriers and cross your own personal dark coral. *Make Your Own Waves* will encourage you to lean into life and commit to its opportunities.

—Shaun Tomson, World Champion surfer,
Author, Speaker, and Entrepreneur

xi

PROLOGUE
THE SURFER'S RULES

CONSIDER THESE:

- ▶ Facebook, the world's largest social media site, creates no content.
- ▶ Wikipedia, the world's most active reference source, employs no scholars.
- ▶ Airbnb, provider of more beds than Hilton and Marriott hotels combined, doesn't own a single mattress.
- ▶ Uber, the world's largest cab company, has zero vehicles.
- ▶ Alibaba, the most valuable global retailer, has no inventory.
- ▶ Skype, the world's largest telephone company, has no telephones.

- Netflix, the world's largest movie house, has no cinemas.
- Reputation.com protects more people from bullying than all local school boards combined, using only algorithms.
- And, Open Table seats more people for dinners than anyone in the world, yet owns no restaurants.

Thanks to the Internet and mobile devices, wave after wave of change keeps coming, and entrepreneurs and innovators have more opportunity than ever to ride them.

This is more than just a surfing metaphor. I have spent much of the last 25 years writing about and researching how serial innovators and entrepreneurs succeed by looking at the mindset, skillset, and toolset they possess, rather than examining only the end product of their endeavors. I have studied the process, not the conclusion—the path, not the destination. I have examined how start-ups can be successful when they replace an "exit strategy" with a "sustainability strategy." I have created a very successful training program, *Innovating for Results,* which offers skills and tools to entrepreneurs, start-ups, and corporations. I have done a deep dive into the world of social entrepreneurs who seek solutions to massive global challenges like disease, hunger, sanitation, and environmental protection to see how they persevere—even thrive—in the face of enormous challenge.

I am also a surfer. I have spent the last 25 years or more speaking to and researching surfers—especially Big Wave surfers—about the enormous challenges, dramatic conditions, and life-or-death experiences they face every time they paddle out into the lineup to take on an approaching wall of water. They are philosophical and wise, as well as deeply knowledgeable about the ocean and what they do. And the steps they follow for a successful ride are the same steps entrepreneurs and innovators need to follow as well. This is why throughout this book I will describe ideas and themes from both the surfer's and the innovator's perspective.

In 1991, I wrote a few pages about "The Surfer's Rules" in my first book, the *New York Times* bestseller *If It Ain't Broke . . . Break It!*[1] In the years since, The Surfer's Rules have evolved and deepened. For this book I gathered information on more than 150 men and women who paddle out into the most challenging conditions imaginable, waves five to ten times taller than their height.

One of the best-known Big Wave surfers in the world is Laird Hamilton. Hamilton pioneered Big Wave riding and tow-in surfing. He's also an entrepreneur who has helped pioneer products such hydrofoil surfboards, stand-up paddleboards, and golf boards, as well as health drinks and fitness programs. His secret?

That was revealed by his wife, volleyball player Gabrielle Reese, in an interview with website POPSUGAR. She was asked, "Do you ever get scared of him being out there [in Big Waves]?"

She said, " . . . Laird's pretty diligent about his preparation and he's actually, believe it or not, very careful. . . . It's a lifetime of being ready for [Big Waves]."[2]

Indeed, being ready for and adjusting to changing conditions is one of the most common skills innovators share with Big Wave surfers.

My research has shown surfers, like innovators, also are comfortable in changing conditions and thrive amidst chaos. Both are able to think like beginners, maintaining "fresh eyes" and an open mind. Since no two waves or opportunities are identical, both pay attention to the "anomalies"—instead of relying on the familiar. Both know that in mastery over the exceptions to the rules, they can make breakthroughs. And

3

they experiment, test, and iterate, whether it's with new processes, products, and services, or new forecasting apps, waxes, fins, and surf spots.

To some, Big Wave surfers may seem like risk takers or adrenaline junkies, but my research shows that like any good entrepreneur, they take *smart* calculated risks and they make astute, quick decisions. To them, adrenaline is related to elation and just helps to stave off fear. Big Wave surfers actually subscribe to the time-tested axiom of carpenters: "Measure twice, cut once." They don't just "roll the dice" and take random chances. They study. They prepare. They remain patient. And then they GO!

Successful innovators and Big Wave surfers also know how to capitalize on their own unique set of strengths. They do not attempt to be what they are not, and they know exactly who they are and what they can offer to a team—and my research shows the most productive teams are built via complementary strengths.

Innovators and entrepreneurs, like Big Wave surfers, are self-confident, which gives them the courage to face the many unanticipated challenges that will come their way. Armed with *un*conventional wisdom, they are better equipped to overcome roadblocks and barriers. Courage and confidence, combined with preparation and practice, unite in a winning combination that can help both groups face daily challenges.

I recently asked South Africa's World Champion surfer Shaun Tomson, "Are there things you learned from surfing that you immediately applied or still apply to business, because you have that experience now of 30 years of various kinds of entrepreneurial activities?"

"I think there's an absolute, direct relationship between surfing and business, in a number of ways," he said. "I think one is that surfing's a solitary sport and you're dependent on your individual powers for success. And whilst business is often conceptualized as a team sport, as teams meshing together in pursuit of common goals, I still think that success or failure (for oneself and in business) depends on one's own actions—in the same way that you paddle out, and that wave comes to you, and then you ride it," Shaun said. "The way you ride it is not dependent on a team, is not dependent on anyone else. And in the same way in business, it's important that you have the support and respect and help of other people, but still you are evaluated on your personal performance."[3]

GoPro executive Steven Baker points out an overarching quality of surfers that innovators and entrepreneurs might recognize in themselves. A boat captain for seven years at the legendary Big Wave mecca Tavarua, Fiji, he had brought many of the world's best XL surfers out into harm's way long before Tavarua was on the global surfing map. I asked Steven to describe the mindset of Big Wave surfers in one sentence.

With no hesitation he succinctly said, "Big Wave surfers are cut from a different cloth than humans."[4]

What makes them different, and what we can learn from them, comprises the 10 chapters that follow. The Surfer's Rules are a 10-step strategic roadmap from start to start-up—then onward to starting anew onto the next opportunity.

Far too many innovators and entrepreneurs veer from (or worse, are completely unaware of) "the basics" and jump two steps ahead of themselves. They want to ride the Big Waves before they even know how to paddle. It's no wonder that 9 out of 10 startups fail.

You have to start at the beginning. And the most basic rule of all is the first one: Learn to swim.

1
LEARN TO
SWIM

"**I**N SURFING, IT'S SO IMPORTANT TO GET THE BASICS DOWN and then take it from there," says pro surfer Jordy Smith. "If your foundation is strong, you'll have all the tools you need to become a well-rounded surfer."[1] On land you learn to crawl, then to walk. On water, you learn to float, then kick, then breathe, then swim, then surf.

I'll give you a quick example of what happens when you skip the first step. I was recently visiting a number of start-ups clustered around one another in a series of buildings called an "Innovation Park." As I walked from office to office and lab to lab, I was introduced to the principals at each company. The passion and high energy in each setting were palpable. One start-up was working on a new design for solar panels that could improve output by as much as 7 percent, a very substantial number in the world of solar energy. They were looking for second-round funding for the "proof of concept" data needed to bring the new design to market.

Just down the hall, I met some people who had breakthrough ideas for computer microchips that could withstand heat of 600+ plus degrees—nearly three times the norm. They were completing their proof of concept phase and had a wealth of information about how to do testing and gather data. As I listened to their explanation of what they were up to, I realized that they had overlapping interests and knowledge with the solar team less than 100 feet down the hall. I asked the microchip team if they were collaborating at all with the solar team and was met with a blank stare. They had no clue as to who was doing what and where. Their offices might as well have been on separate continents.

I tell this story to further make a case for the "clean slate" being a good place to start. To most, it's common sense to know how to swim before entering the ocean. But to many entrepreneurs and start-ups, the basics are often not obvious at all. A major part of mastering the basics in the world of work is knowing what the basics are in your given situation and how they are changing: the trends, the competition, the metrics people find useful, the strengths of your team, and your product's full potential. It also includes knowing what is going on a few feet down the hall.

As an entrepreneur, it's also important that as you grow you keep learning, adjusting, and modifying. One size does not fit all. As they say in surfing, you outgrow your board.

"I was fortunate enough to have my dad as my [board] shaper, but I definitely had a few growth spurts where I got too big for the board I was riding at the time," Jordy Smith says. The changes and modifications to a board can be simple and inexpensive at various growth stages, such as switching to a different fin but keeping the same board. Eventually, though, you will outgrow your board and be ready for the next iteration—or, more often, ocean conditions will dictate what equipment you need.

Surfer or innovator, as you grow and mature, the modifications you make are never set in stone. There is no set recipe, but there are many healthy ingredients from which to choose. One of the most basic skills is knowing when it is time to replace the old with the new.

For example, former pro-surfer Conan Hayes noticed the toll of age and injury on even the best surfers on the World Tour given the repetitive nature of their lives, the injuries, the arduous travel, and the long periods on the road. Looking for a fresh start on his own terms and timing, Hayes co-founded RVCA (pronounced "roo-cah") lifestyle apparel in 2001. RVCA quickly became a hit with surfers and skateboarders everywhere. After selling RVCA to Billabong in 2010, Hayes continued on his journey out of the water.[2]

Or consider Kelly Slater, surfing's iconic double-digit World Champion. I saw a T-shirt once that read: "Jordan + Kobe = Slater." This is a reference to the fact that Slater has more world titles than Michael Jordan and Kobe Bryant combined. Yet even Slater aged over time, so, like Conan Hayes, he has been involved in several business ventures and social causes—most recently the sustainable men's clothing company Outerknown, man-made wave pools and Slater Designs high-tech surfboards.

THE BIGGER THE WAVE, THE HARDER YOU PREPARE

I live about 30 miles north of one of the most famous and dangerous Big Wave surf spots in the world, Maverick's. Big Wave surfers come from far and near when Maverick's is "on," and entire books have been written about its unique history.[3]

When I think of Maverick's, I think of two Big Wave surfers in particular. The first is Jeff Clark, who blazed the trail at Maverick's and was the first to surf it. (More about Jeff later.) The other is the late Santa Cruz, CA, surfer Jay Moriarity.

Although I'm not a Big Wave surfer myself, on many occasions I would stop by Maverick's and get vicariously pumped up by the men and women riding the giants there. Late one afternoon in 1994, I finished a project in the Silicon Valley and decided to swing by Maverick's to clear my head and see what was happening.

It was a typical Northern California fall day: overcast, windy, and about 52 degrees in and out of the water, with swells of two to-four feet. I drove past the small Pillar Point Harbor and turned down the road that winds its way to the dirt parking area. From there it is about a half-mile walk to the beach.

As I reached the water's edge, a young surfer who I'd never met came towards me carrying his nine-foot board. I said, "Hi, I'm Lou." "Hi," he said, "I'm Jay."

I asked him about the surfing, starting with the usual, "How goes it out there?" "Oh," he said with his great smile, "I didn't surf at all today. I just paddled around the point and back." We talked for a couple of minutes, enough for me to find out he paddled every chance he got (and that's after a full day at high school and a long drive to Maverick's from Santa Cruz, CA). He told me some of the landmarks of his paddle, and we soon said our goodbyes. When I got back to my car I pulled out a map from the glove compartment and checked out exactly where his landmarks were. I did some quick calculations and determined that he had just paddled *12 miles*!

At the time, I did not know who he was, or the legend Jay Moriarity would rightly become. But I have never forgotten the lesson I learned from him about the basics: The training. The commitment. The discipline. How facing the joys and challenges of Big Waves, much like starting a business, takes a commensurate amount of hard work and preparation. That's also part of learning to swim.

BETTER THAN LUCKY

Today's business world contains many surfer entrepreneurs who succeeded because they paid attention to basics in order to create blockbuster products. Consider these success stories:

Nick Woodman had a penchant for making action videos and taking still photos in the water. At times frustrated by having only two God-given hands, Woodman would duct tape his 35mm camera to his arm as he ventured out. Realizing that others shared his frustration, he borrowed some money from his mother, experimented with prototypes, tested, and revised until he had created a breakthrough and affordable new kind of camera. He is the billionaire founder and creator of the GoPro.

Not too far away from Nick Woodman, Bob McKnight had an idea for a retail clothing line. Driving up and down the coast of California, from the back of his Volkswagen bus he *gave away* his fledgling company's versatile boardshorts to beachgoers as a way to get media attention. As his clothing line started to take off, he continued his guerrilla marketing tactics by sponsoring sporting events rather than using normal print and TV advertising channels. Thus was born Quiksilver, where he now serves as executive chairman. And, not resting on his laurels, when he noticed an untapped market for young, active girls clothing he launched what is now the largest action sport brand for young women, Roxy, naming it after his daughter.

Halfway around the world from Bob McKnight, Argentine brothers Fernando and Santiago Aguerre noticed that most shoes were not designed with warm or wet weather in mind, and rarely held up well for active people in tough weather conditions. Traditional sandals were not of sufficient quality or fit, and inexpensive flip-flops lasted about a week at a time. Seizing an opportunity, sturdy and long-lasting Reef footwear was born.

Though separated by thousands of miles and representing different industries, these three stories have two things in common: all trace their business roots to what they learned from surfing, and all started from the ground up.

As any amped-up entrepreneur will tell you, the power of bringing an idea to market is euphoric, and to be able to do it repeatedly is addictive. Like Big Wave surfer Dusty Payne and those other professional Big Wave surfers who are able to devote all their time and energy to surfing know, their basic preparation has made them "better than lucky."

"WHY DON'T I LIKE FLY-FISHING?"

Beyond the media circus that surrounds the so-called surfers "laid-back lifestyle," these are men and women who grew up facing changing ocean conditions daily and learned lessons that transcend the sport—about life, about themselves, and about how preparation expedites opportunities to succeed.

If you look closely at the Big Wave surfers, you can see a mindset, skillset, and toolset that would serve any entrepreneur or innovator well. To "those who ride giants," Big Wave surfing is more a "calling" than a sport, . . . an irresistible passion comparable to the energy found in every innovation lab and start-up anywhere in the world—a calling that totally consumes you in spite of the obstacles and dangers.

Big wave champion surfer Grant Washburn describes this feeling well. "Some mornings I wake up and hear those 20-second intervals [between massive waves] booming from in front of my house, and I lay there and think to myself, 'Why don't I like fly-fishing? Or sailing? Or something else—anything else.'"[4] To Washburn, when the surf's up nothing is more compelling.

SURFER STEP

1

LEARN TO SWIM

What comes before the start-up, invention, or new product? Many would-be entrepreneurs face incredible self-imposed barriers to entry that they can avoid by taking the simplest of first steps. Basic research, networking, and prototyping are essential. Without those first baby steps your dream is at risk.

Nine out of 10 start-ups fail, and in my research and experience 9 out of 10 times they fail because they try to bypass the basics. So, where does an innovator start? In the beginning, there is work to be done on three levels: the mindset, the skillset and the toolset. The mindset gives you the ideas and strategies. The skillset gets you moving towards gathering resources needed for implementation. And the toolset helps you to refine and execute. Taken together they are like three legs of a stool; they create stability.

Jeff Amerine is a successful entrepreneur many times over. Based in Northwest Arkansas, for 25 years he has been involved in the investor community as well, so he knows both sides of the equation. He and I have done TV interviews and podcasts together focusing on innovation and entrepreneurship because we share the same desire and perspective—

13

hard work and good preparation make success much more likely. Most recently, Jeff has created Startup Junkie, a consulting practice that coaches, mentors, and advises startups regarding venture finance, business model validation, and growth strategies—the entrepreneurial equivalent of learning to swim.

THINGS TO DO:

It's important to start with the basics. As I do in my Innovating for Results Workshop, ask the following fundamental questions:

1. What business am I in?

2. What *other* businesses am I in?

3. Am I maximizing, leveraging, and aligning the benefits of all my businesses?

For example, at first most automobile dealerships believed they were in the business of selling cars. But when looking at where their revenue comes from, they realized they were also in the automotive financing and insurance business. The revenue from leasing, interest on monthly payments, and selling extended warranties exceeded the profit from car sales. When dealers realized this, they developed business plans to maximize all lines of business.

2
GET WET

"**I**F IT'S BREAKING, YOU'RE OUT THERE. YOU DON'T NEED much," says Australian pro-surfer Julian Wilson. "A wave that spills is enough. It's all about getting salty. There's always an excuse, but we all know how good we feel after a surf."[1]

There are people who look like surfers, dress like surfers, and talk like surfers, but they never get in the water. It sounds simple, but it's true—being in the ocean is not the same as being on the beach. There is nothing vicarious about surfing . . . or business. You have to get wet to be where the action is.

Similarly, in the business world, there are people who talk and look the part of entrepreneurs and innovators but who have nothing to show for all those great ideas and dreams because they never muster the courage to stick a toe in the water, let alone dive in.

You might sympathize with them. The marketplace is, after all, like the ocean. It's wild and uncertain. The wind blows hard. The currents are relentless, the swells are endless, and riptides threaten to sweep you away. As Big Wave surfer Mark Healey says, "Anytime you step into the ocean, you're in an environment that's completely uncontrolled by humans." It's no wonder many swimmers prefer to lay on a towel and catch some rays. But Healey also says, "Everyone needs to connect with that sort of wildness in some way, especially in a time when there's so much noise and distraction in our daily lives."[2] In the world of business, your willingness to touch the wild and unpredictable marketplace, to make that commitment, is what separates you as special.

Consider what an entrepreneur's life is like compared to that of the salaried employee.

EMPLOYEES	ENTREPRENEURS
A steady paycheck	A deferred paycheck
Predictable work hours	All-consuming work hours
Routine work assignments	Changing work projects
Familiar co-workers	Varying collaborators
Constant work environment	Flexible workspaces

Being an entrepreneur is not for everyone. But you don't necessarily have to go it alone. You can be an intrapreneur, an entrepreneur *within* a large company. You can also affiliate with organizations like The Unreasonable Institute to help you tackle social problems in an entrepreneurial way. You don't have to create a startup from scratch. You do, though, have to somehow get your feet wet.

Garrett McNamara is among a very elite group of Big Wave surfers who have been towed in and ridden waves estimated at

80 to 100 feet high. The video of him riding one of the biggest waves on record at Nazaré, Portugal, went viral and had nearly nine million views.[3] Even at his level, he had to decide when to leave the beach and head into the water. His attitude is so simple that we can all learn from it: "You just have to get out there to feel it, to get to know it."[4]

SURF WITH THE AMATEURS

We all have excuses and self-imposed barriers. We can come up with dozens of reasons to stay on the beach. And just as we construct barriers in our own heads, companies have an arsenal of roadblocks, as well. As Intuit co-founder Scott Cook said when interviewed about innovation, "Normally, companies put up a phalanx of barriers and hurdles and mountains to climb that may not seem hard for the boss or the CEO but are intensely hard, impossibly hard, for our young innovator to conquer. So our job as leaders is—how do we get all those barriers out of the way?"[5]

The surf community has always pushed boundaries and sought to keep things interesting. Within the culture, free expression is encouraged and at most local beach breaks there are special spots for the "groms" (children) and beginners. Fathers and mothers teach their daughters and sons to enjoy the special power of the ocean. They teach the basics of positioning, paddling, dropping in, and pulling out. And with more time in the water, the novice will start to learn the "rules" of the game created over many decades by the surfing community. As South African World Champion Big Wave surfer Shaun Tomson says in his book *Surfer's Code*, "All surfers are joined by one ocean. You aren't alone in wanting to get off the beach. There are many who'll help you get wet and make sure you don't founder."[6]

You'll also learn the unwritten rules of the sport. As Rob Gilley wrote in *Surfer* magazine, "Perhaps one of the greatest things about the pursuit of surfing is the lack of regimentation. No need to reserve court time, buy a lift ticket, or wait for the ref to show up—just grab your stick and go. Even the act itself is usually pretty loose—no governing body monitoring you and no authority figures telling you what to do. We surf by an informal collection of unspoken/unwritten 'rules' that wave riders learn about over time."[7] The same holds for being an innovator or entrepreneur. I know of no rulebook, entry ticket requirement, or sanctioning body.

Unwritten rules are much harder to learn and far easier to break. As surf lineups get more crowded and the potential for conflicts rises, a number of surfers have tried to put something in writing. Easier said than done. For example, some surfers have already posted a list of rules at their local breaks. In California, as Gilley says, "You might have noticed unofficial signs fronting several reef and point breaks along the coast. Most of these mini-billboards were posted by locals in the wake of the '90s beginner boom, when unknowing novices began to breach the unwritten rules of the lineup."[8]

It helps to follow the unwritten rules for entrepreneurs, too, so you don't kill a great opportunity because of a breach of etiquette. For example, your "pitch" to investors needs to be brief and compelling. Your ability to monetize your idea must be clear and viable. And your "exit or sustainability strategy" must be as well thought through as your entrance plan. If none of these bases are covered, you will be dismissed quickly in the marketplace.

Not every expert follows the rules, though. Just as there are naysayers in the business world who will try to exploit your weaknesses and play on your fears, some surfers can be total assholes. Aaron James, a surfer and best-selling author of *Assholes: A Theory*, said the following in an interview with *Surfer* magazine:

"I first got the idea of defining the term 'asshole' in the water while watching a guy blatantly burn someone and then get angry at the victim when he complained. We grow up dealing with this a lot, but this was the first time I had a philosophical moment with it."[9]

James, a Harvard-educated PhD philosophy professor, used this epiphany and "thought it would be fun to try to define what the moral type is, because a philosopher is supposed to define what is otherwise obscure."[10]

James defines an asshole as "a person that allows himself to enjoy special advantages in interpersonal relations out of an entrenched sense of entitlement that immunizes him against the complaints of other people."

That's the definition he proposes and is "based on the surfer who repeatedly snakes people and then yells at them when they reasonably complain."[11]

So, prepare for assholes as you would for a riptide: know that they're surprising, possibly terrifying, but quite manageable if you keep your cool.

And take heart. Most surfers know the difference between a novice and an asshole. Some even value beginners for their enthusiasm and perspectives. When Bob Hurley, founder of the surf company Hurley Sports, starts to run out of ideas, he thinks back to something that happened many years ago on Huntington Beach when he was an avid surfer himself. Liz Wiseman writes in her book *Rookie Smarts*, "He ran into Wayne Bartholomew, the reigning world champion surfer at the time, who said he preferred surfing with beginners because they gave him energy . . . So Bob told me, 'Now when I have bad days, I go out and surf with the amateurs.' He spends his time talking to them, hanging out with them, and he says it revitalizes his point of view."[12]

19

FEAR MAY BE JUST WHAT THE
DOCTOR ORDERED

A more common barrier to leaving the beach is our own fear. For many, those first moments in the ocean—as well as in the marketplace—can be scary. Even a small wave near the shore can give you a decent respect for the power of the surf and the reality of a strong undertow. For some, that is when they head back to the beach. Others, whether they're surfers or entrepreneurs, make adjustments of the body and mind and face their fears.

Few moments in Big Wave surfing are as scary as falling from a freakish large wave only to realize that the one behind it will pound you as you surface for air. It matters little if you are Brazil's preeminent female Big Wave surfer Maya Gabeira at Nazaré on a 60-foot colossus or a local guy on his first wave—riding waves is scary.

But behavioral science has proven that fear has counter-intuitive benefits. As it turns out, fear can be good for you. Researchers have studied the long-term effects of stress and fear and there is recent evidence that our bodies actually—and absolutely—love short-term stresses in the face of danger.

Firdaus Dhabhar is a professor of behavioral science at Stanford University. For two decades, he has been looking at how high levels of acute short-term stress affect the body. Recent data has shown that "freaking out in the face of danger supercharges the immune system, sending beneficial cells to places most likely to be injured, everything from the skin, the lungs, and the gut." There's even some evidence that stress-charged immune cells could effectively fight cancerous tumors. "It may not work," Dhabhar says about figuring out how to use stress hormones to fight cancer, "but if it did the benefits could be tremendous."[13]

More interesting still, Dhabhar's colleagues at Stanford are showing that hormones in the brain can actually improve memory and learning under short-term stress. "Stress has a very bad reputation. It's in pretty bad shape, PR-wise," acknowledges Dhabhar. But, adds Conor Liston of Rockefeller University, "If you think of stress in terms of arousal—being awake and alert and oriented to changes in the environment—this is a good thing for learning."[14]

It turns out riding that first Big Wave and overcoming your fears also has some fringe benefits, even for Big Wave surfers: "What happened to me with Maverick's," says Grant "Twig" Baker, "was that I got there and my first day out there was a perfect day . . . I just fell in love with the wave."[15] So, stress has its benefits that can overtake fears and lead to increased commitment and desire, useful traits for any entrepreneur.

A TIME TO "DO" AND "UNDO"

Dr. Timothy Leary is even more "zen," as he once discussed on now-defunct website the *Stoke Report*: " . . . (t)he surfer is dealing with the most basic elements of all. There's almost no technology, and there's no symbolism. It's just the individual dealing with the power of the ocean . . . There's purity about surfing. There's a great sense of timing . . . timing is of absolute importance," he says. "Being in the right place at the right time—it happens that whatever you do, you can't create a wave . . . it comes and there's a time to move and a time to lay back."[16]

Whether you are a surfer or an innovator in the workplace, timing matters. There is a time to "do" and a time to "undo." As Anne Lamott, one of my favorite writers and people, says, "Almost everything will work again if you unplug it for a few minutes, including you."[17] So when the time is right, unplug from the beach, head into the water, and enjoy getting wet.

GET WET

In business, what can you do to leave the comfort of a salaried job and a secure schedule to venture into the world of the entrepreneur? It starts with knowing yourself and knowing your comfort level with ambiguity, even chaos. Then you can certainly do your due diligence about your ideas. You can network with potential collaborators. You can find supportive mentors. And you can anticipate and face your fears.

A recent article about start-ups on McKinsey & Company's website offers advice: "How should you tap into Silicon Valley? Not by sticking a toe in the water. Get your management team aligned and then commit."[18] Commitment cannot be underrated nor faked. An investor told me once that he is not fond of simulations or anything theoretical. When he recently was asked to teach a business school seminar on entrepreneurship, he practiced what he preached. His course offered no set syllabus. Instead, he formed three student teams and lured them into entrepreneurial waters by giving them each $1,000 and telling them to go start a business. Their businesses were tracked for the whole semester, and students reported weekly on their obstacles and victories. He made them instant entrepreneurs who had to walk the talk. For the committed entrepreneur there is no better "training" than doing.

The ocean, like the marketplace, is ever-changing, so you have to assess the conditions before you get wet. It's no surprise the same ocean that inspires surfers to ride waves also inspires them to become entrepreneurs and make a living related to what they love. That's why so many surf-related companies have been founded that enable surfers to earn a living on their passions.

"Sure, 'rely' on the ocean is one way to put it," says Neil Anthony Sims, co-founder and CEO of Kampachi Farms LLC in Kona, "But 'live, breath, love and pray for' the ocean might be more exact." For many, getting in the water is a transformative experience. "It's ever-changing, it's unpredictable," says Miguel "Micco" Godinez, the co-owner of the Hanalei-based Kayak Kauai, an adventure tour company. In 1980, Godinez and his brother Chino literally kayaked for five months from Seattle to Skagway, Alaska. During this trip they first envisioned their company, and then the hard work began. Four years later, they founded Kayak Kauai. "The company has grown from just offering kayak tours to renting bikes, giving surfing and stand-up paddling lessons, guiding hikes along the Na Pali Coast, and taking visitors on sea kayaks to watch the migrating humpback whales along the island's southern coast."

"From May to August, all I do is sleep and go to work," he says. "But no complaints."[19]

In order to reap the rewards of venturing into the marketplace, entrepreneurs have to get their fingernails dirty. For entrepreneurs, the rewards may be money or a sense of achievement; for surfers it's the rush of adrenaline when they paddle out and face new and unpredictable challenges.

THINGS TO DO:

When you have an idea or invention that you want to take to market, there are a number of early-stage issues to explore. Perhaps the most important one is asking yourself, "Are you ready to be an entrepreneur and leave the safety and security of your work life?" Rate the following questions on a scale of 1-10, with 10 being the highest:

1. How important is a fixed salary to you?

2. How important is a set work schedule?

3. Do you thrive when your roles and responsibilities are not well-defined?

4. Do you have a support network to advise and encourage you?

5. How willing are you to incur personal debt in order to grow your business?

If your score is 40 or below, it may be that the life of the entrepreneur is not for you.

3
DECIDE
TO RIDE

ONCE YOU HAVE LEARNED TO GET WET AND SWIM, MANY more decisions await about what to *do* in the water. It's one thing to watch people catching waves from the beach, where it looks so easy. It's another to be in that churning ocean and decide to ride.

Over coffee one afternoon, Shaun Tomson told me, "Surfing's very similar to business and it's very similar to being an entrepreneur. An entrepreneur is gonna get up in the morning and take on the day. And you don't have a company and thousands of people around you to support you," he said. "And if you want to be a successful entrepreneur you're very much dealing with 'the next wave.' And you're dealing with being able to be creative and innovative. And when I approached my surfing that was how I was. I tried to be creative. I tried to be imaginative. I tried to ride my own way. I tried to have my own style. I tried to think about waves and how to ride them differently. So everything that I learned in my surfing career and in my surfing as an artist—riding a wave is a very artistic endeavor—I used in my business endeavors."[1]

For the entrepreneur, the main "decisions" are often tied to the gathering of resources. Resources take many forms: the right opportunity, the necessary capital to move forward, the appropriate market research, the strategic business plan, and most importantly, the right people in the right places. Decisions are informed by the mindset, skillset, and toolset at your disposal. "There's a lot of guys who want it. It's insane to sit there on the beach," says Reef McIntosh, winner of the Oakley Wave of the Winter contest.[2]

There is no entry fee required to make decisions. No waiting period or formal education is needed. The start button is conveniently located inside your gut. We all started out—as everyone does when facing the challenge of their first wave or first business—low on expertise, high on tenacity, and strong on aspirations. And I will tell you a secret from my experience—being a novice has its disadvantages, but it also has its advantages.

Naïveté has its place. "My real value didn't come from having fresh ideas. It was having no ideas at all," says Bob Hurley, founder of Hurley Sports. "When you know nothing, you're forced to create something . . . I have a whole set of scars that remind me not to do things that didn't seem to work out very well the first time. You also have to realize that you will have ideas that touch on other people's scar tissue. They will quickly say, 'No, no, we tried that and it didn't work.' This is a major way that experience can create a number of troubling blind spots."[3]

*Un*conventional wisdom has taught me that your past experience can also slow you down. "You know," says Lorraine Twohill, Google's senior vice president of global marketing, "it's not a two-year lead time for a Google product. It's much quicker.

Being able to bring consumer insights to the table in real time and get insights back in—being able to test and iterate, test and iterate—is extremely important." She adds, "The way I think about marketing—and the way I tend to talk to my team about it—is knowing the user, knowing the magic, and connecting the two."[4] There is a certain magic in having "fresh eyes."

Big Wave surfers approach each ride with a mixture of all their experiences that led up to the moment, the amazing ability to *not* think once they commit to a wave, and the chance to relish the magic of the moment. Part of accessing this magic comes from keeping things simple.

IT'S JUST H$_2$O!

The surf at Maverick's, near Half Moon Bay, CA, is among the most challenging in the world. One of the most respected surfers there is Santa Cruz's Darryl "Flea" Virostko. Winner three straight times at the Maverick's surf competition, Flea is known as a fearless surfer with a special passion for this surf spot who describes himself as "one of the last of the pioneers." Among the first to ride Maverick's waves, he was hooked from day one. As one of the earliest to test himself there, Flea ventured where very few had gone before, always going full throttle. "The energy I got right when I paddled out is like, I get goose bumps right now talking about it, because it's something that goes through my blood . . . There's people that 'charge' Maverick's and there's people that 'surf' Maverick's and people who charge, win."[5]

I remember being in the crowd for all of Flea's Maverick's victories. At one, I was standing close to Flea when a fan approached him. The fan was holding a color postcard of what I assume was a picture of Flea on a huge 40-foot-plus wave, making him look very much like a small flea on a big dog. There was something ominous about the scale of man-to-wave in the photo.

The fan was seeking an autograph, and handed Flea a blue Sharpie and the postcard. They exchanged a few words, Flea wrote something, signed the card, and walked on. Years later while perusing surfing memorabilia on eBay, I saw for sale what may have been that card, and I bought it.

I never imagined that the few words Flea wrote could capture so succinctly the tenacity and the magic of Big Wave riders. He said: "It's just H_2O!—FLEA."

Literally, ever since then, I can't tell you how many times I have thought of Flea when a big decision or opportunity faces me and said to myself, "It's just business!"

The world of business has its own Fleas who face massive challenges and turn them into opportunities. Thousands of articles and blogs have chronicled the game-changing innovators who faced stiff competition and against all odds, emerged victorious. The media has put a select few business pioneers like Steve Jobs, Elon Musk, and Jack Dorsey on a pedestal, but my experience and research have shown that innovation most often happens not when it's left to the "chosen few" but rather when it is part of everybody's everyday job.

My second book, *Don't Compete . . . TILT! The Field*,[6] looked at innovators from the perspective of forging ahead into unchartered waters, unfazed by the naysayers and skeptics who want to "firehose" your ideas. In it, I showed that the best innovators are those who are not focused on beating the competition. Quite the contrary, they seek to create a new field rather than compete for a share of a pre-existing one. Chef Michel Nischan of Wholesome Wave says, "Hurdles aren't hurdles, they're just a turn in the road you didn't expect . . . You can't be afraid to move when you don't have all the answers, or you'll never get anywhere."[7]

Like Flea, Sheryl Sandberg, COO of Facebook, epitomizes the "decide-to-ride" and go-for-it attitude of innovators. If she were to autograph someone's card, I could imagine her writing one of my favourite quotes she's said: "If you're offered a seat on a rocket ship, don't ask what seat! Just get on."[8]

WATCH THE LINEUP

In the language of surfing, the "lineup" refers to the area where the waves start to break and where most surfers wait to catch a wave. Watching the behavior in the lineup will offer many clues on technique, conditions and etiquette. So, once you decide you want to surf and paddle out into the lineup, one of the first things to "do" is . . . *nothing.* Sit on your board a while. Watch. Listen. Observe. Learn.

In an article entitled "What Surfing Can Teach You About Entrepreneurship," Nicholas Mohnacky says, "When it comes to understanding a new surf break, you can read guides, charts, reports, and local resources, but hands down, the best way to get a spot dialed in is to watch other surfers at that spot. Take a few minutes to . . . see where riders are taking off, watch where they're high-lining, stalling, or hitting the lip on the closeout sections. Familiarity with a particular surf spot could mean the difference between life and death."[9] Taking time to watch the lineup in the marketplace could make or break your business, too. It's the kind of awareness and patience that requires diligence and astute attention to detail.

"Today's Big Wave surfers aren't just thrill-seekers. They're also scientists, storm chasers, amateur meteorologists armed with radar, swell charts, buoy readings," says John Gustafson. "Winter storms that kick up around Alaska's Aleutian Islands and head south are particularly intriguing. On radar they appear as massive purple or magenta blobs, and the trick is to predict where and when the swells produced by said blobs will hit."[10]

In business, as in surfing, it is important to do your homework and pay attention to the details in order to maximize the results. This is how Laird Hamilton helped pioneer tow-in surfing.

THE BEST LEARN FROM THE WISE

As chronicled in *Club of the Waves*,[11] Laird found going to Hawaiian schools difficult because he was one of a very few white/blonde kids—a "haole," as the locals say. So Laird looked to an older generation of surfers who were at the time pioneering short-board Pipeline masters and Big Wave surfers, including his step-father Billy. Never one to be complacent, he became a great Pipeline surfer and also started to experiment with bigger, faster waves, made possible by his knowledge of the physics of windsurfing.

Through part-time modeling, Laird met pro surfer Buzzy Kerbox. Together they experimented in wakeboarding by using a rubber zodiac boat, a towrope, and a surfboard. This led the two, along with Darrick Doerner, to try the same thing with bigger waves in more challenging ocean conditions.

"Inspired also by the short strap-in boards used in snowboarding, Laird, with the help of surfboard shapers Dick Brewer, Billy Hamilton, and Gerry Lopez, designed a shorter board with foot straps. And so tow-in surfing was born. In time, the zodiac was replaced by the jet-ski (for speed and mobility), and Laird would continue to push the boundaries . . ."[12]

In 2000 he towed in to huge waves previously unknown and/or un-ridden at Tavarua; Fiji; Pe'ahi, Maui (aka Jaws), Hawaii; and Teahupo'o (pronounced "cho-pu") in Tahiti, which breaks over a very shallow and dangerous coral reef. His fearless approach to Big Wave riding has earned him the respect and admiration of surfers around the world because he is not afraid to innovate and try the untried.

TENACITY TRUMPS TALENT

You might think, "That's great, but he's Laird Hamilton." Indeed, some have argued that surfing is akin to a God-given gift that only the chosen few can accomplish. That could not be farther from the truth. In Big Wave surfing, as in launching a successful start-up, the key differentiator is often the willingness to do the hard work.

I have had conversations with venture capitalists about this very thing. I ask them if a strong work ethic is part of what they look for before investing in companies. The answer is consistent: brains and talent aren't enough. They look for tenacity and passion, because those traits attract other smart people. They would take someone who's willing to work hard over someone with a lot of formal education—preferring someone who knows what it's like to make ends meet over someone with a large inheritance

Succinct advice like this is available at all stages, because you never stop learning. I was at the Oakley Lowers Pro competition watching a heat in which Kelly Slater started on a wave late but paddled extra-hard and caught a high-scoring wave. Via loudspeakers that allowed attendees to hear the live television feed, I heard this gem from the commentator: "99% of surfing is paddling!" A high percentage of being a successful entrepreneur often boils down to out-paddling the competition.

In my more than 25 years in the world of start-ups, one of the things I have noticed about the successful ones is that their founders model what to do and how to do it. And what is the difference between successful entrepreneurs and unsuccessful ones? Successful entrepreneurs do all the things unsuccessful people don't want to do, like making hard decisions or letting go of talented people who aren't performing.

Most people don't want to work more hours than they have to. They do the minimum they are paid to do. That's not the way to get ahead as an entrepreneur—or in surfing. You may be developing a new technology or invention, but you also have to know the history of your products, keep a critical eye on budget, solicit constant feedback, and yes, even take out the trash sometimes. And you have to be prepared to do this over and over again.

As Garrett James writes in a *Surfer* magazine article titled "Kelly Slater Is His Own Biggest Critic," "You don't become 11-time World Champ without analyzing every little aspect of your surfing. The fact of the matter: Kelly Slater has been filming, watching, and correcting his surfing since before half of the Top 34 (pro surfers) were in grade school."[13]

THE DEVILS—AND THE ANGELS—ARE IN THE DETAILS

In large measure, when you decide to ride waves big or small, details matter. Consider world-class Big Wave surfer Greg Long, the only surfer to win Maverick's Surf Contest, the Red Bull Rider's Cup (at Dungeons), the WSL Big Wave competition, and the Quiksilver in Memory of Eddie Aikau (known as "The Eddie"). The son of a lifeguard, he was raised knowing how little things can get you into and/or out of trouble. Attention to detail is his way of facing fear.

The fear factor is ever-present in business as in the ocean, and being prepared is how Long deals with the fear of riding waves as tall as redwood trees. "There was a time when I wanted to see how big of a wave could I ride, how scary of a situation could I put myself in and still have control of the way I react to that situation," he says. "As twisted as that sounds to some people, there's no other way to put it. It's empowering. You learn to control your mind; you control the world and the reality around you."

"So what you learn from facing fear head on," says Long, is that "what it demands of you, what it shows you are the places that you need to grow within this concept of fear, which is what really keeps people from realizing their greatest potential in this world."[14] Known for his meticulous preparation, he has backups for his backups! For him, the devils—and the angels—are in the details.

Dane Reynolds is a surfer's surfer. He has the respect of his colleagues, young and old. As the late surfing legend Andy Irons said of him, "Dane's surfing is epic—it's just so raw and original. He puts his board in places where you can see his body reacting to the wave. He responds to it; he's not trying to force anything, he just makes things happen. The best surfers ever are guys who do that, they ride the wave the way it is supposed to be ridden. Guys like (Tom) Curren did that, and I think Dane one of the few young surfers who can do it."[15]

When Dane surfs, time almost stands still. His rides are effortless. His joy is obvious. He easily gets "in the zone." Laird Hamilton describes the zone this way: "When you see a big one. And seize it. And get on it. Everything else ceases to exist."[16]

Shawn Dollar says, "Surfing big waves is the biggest challenge, takes like all elements, like mentally, physically . . . like everything you've learned to go surf a Big Wave. It's really fun to push yourself and try to catch one of those things." And to Dollar, above all else, "The rad-est thing is every Big Wave surfer out there is doing it because they love it."[17] Surfers like John John Florence and the late Brock Little exude that love and pure joy. Words of wisdom for the aspiring entrepreneur:

The old cliché holds true, love it or leave it. The old cliché holds true: love it or leave it.

I asked Titans of Mavericks champion Big Wave surfer Nic Lamb about the first time he decided to ride the giants. As was the case with most of the Big Wave legends like Ross Clarke-Jones, the decision to go big took time. "It was somewhat gradual. When I was about 4, 5, or 6 my father took me out into waves that really, really scared me. I remember being so scared, and it wasn't really that big, 6-7-foot, and I remember coming out and crying to my mom 'I'm never gonna go out there and do that again.' I hated it! And then, about 5 or 6 years later when I was around 12, something just clicked and switched and I gravitated towards larger surf," he said. "And pushing myself I got more and more comfortable and at 13, 14 I was surfing bigger waves than most grown men around me. I was moving further and further north up the coast. It had always been a dream of mine to surf Maverick's and I didn't stop until I got there. I was 14 or 15 . . . I believe I was a year younger than when Jay (Moriarity) first rode there. I went up there with a friend and my father and it was about 15 foot. And the waves were like sleigh rides, I was just buzzing! I couldn't get enough of it."[18] A dozen years later he was the Maverick's champion.

Entrepreneurs will tell you the same thing. John James, MD and CEO of Hayseed Ventures, decided to be an entrepreneur at a young age. He paid his way through medical school by selling cowboy boots from his dorm room, and surprised himself when he realized that he had figured out how to sell online. He knew that with that knowledge he could sell anything he wanted, especially products that were a bit off the beaten path of mainstream retailers. He didn't have all the answers when he ventured into business, but he knew enough to launch his first one. That led to selling nursing shoes and then opening online stores such as All Around Dance, Hectic Gourmet, The Mom,

The Baby Habit, Ruby Canvas, Fat Chance, Top Slugger, and Scrubsy. Eventually though, like deciding to surf over other options in the ocean, he realized that he had too many companies. He had to decide which of them to ride, and selling cowboy boots via his Country Outfitters store rose to the top.

DECIDE TO RIDE

Surfing is a series of decisions, and so is being an entrepreneur. Most people don't *have* to venture out into uncertain conditions without a steady income or a monthly paycheck. So some will opt for more security and certainty. But for those entrepreneurs and innovators who "decide to ride," the rewards exceed the risks, and breakthroughs come from overcoming limits.

For example, just imagine if you were a young girl surfer . . . from India . . . where there are few surfers . . . and even fewer who are female. Having a design school background, Suhasini Damian teamed up with a friend to start a surfboard bag and swimwear brand, 4Shore. When asked why she decided to make swimwear and board bags, she said, "After I graduated from the design school, we decided to make swimwear because where I live there is a market for it but no supplier. Since [her boyfriend] shapes boards for Indi and since I am a tailor, they asked us to make Indi board bags for them. We make customized swimwear, as well, and that's our specialty."[19]

As in surfing, the "decision" to be an entrepreneur entails overcoming constraints and being ready to put stability and security on the proverbial back burner. The decision is also

35

often tied to gathering resources and building on your idea via collaboration with others.

For the innovator, as for the surfer, the decision is often iterative. It takes small and frequent changes to a model or idea, and it is at this stage when things like prototyping, re-designing, and tinkering take front stage. But at this point to ride or not to ride is no longer at issue—the decision has been made, and you are *almost* good to go.

THINGS TO DO:

This is a time to take a first pass at describing what it is you want to do from an array of options. You have to prioritize and make some fundamental decisions. Use the following process to get started.

Assemble your key stakeholders and spend a full day discussing the following questions. Record the entire day's discussion so that no thought or idea is lost.

1. Where am I in the development of my product or service? Am I good-to-go or do I need more time?

2. What is my revenue model going to be? How will I bring in more friends, followers, and most importantly, funds?

3. How will I sell my idea, product, or service?

4. Do I have the necessary resources and people?

Review and analyze the information from the day and then formulate a two-to-three page "Draft Business Plan."

4

ALWAYS
LOOK
"OUTSIDE"

WHEN YOU WANT SOMETHING SO BADLY THAT YOU CAN
almost taste it, you are often the least likely person to
know if you are really ready and if the time is right. Though
you don't need to have "all" the data, information, or paper-
work in place, it is important to have *many* things done before
you launch.

The previous chapters spelled out a sequence to the way Big
Wave surfers thrive. They move from the basics of swimming,
to stepping into the ocean, to decing what among many choices
they will do in the water. Innovators, entrepreneurs, and start-
ups succeed in the same way. They learn the basics, head into
the marketplace, and decide on their niche. So, what comes
next? You take one more look "outside."

Before you commit to paddling to catch a wave, I was taught to "always look outside." In other words, "outside" refers to looking at the waves in the set *behind* the wave closest to you. Surfers will also yell "*Outside!*" as a warning to other surfers that a bigger wave is coming and it may break further out. If you simply go for the first wave, you may miss a better opportunity—or worse, you may put yourself in danger. In business I see the failure to look "outside" all the time: entrepreneurs get so antsy to get something to market, they have no clue of bigger and better opportunities that are there if they could just wait a bit more and leave the low-hanging fruit to others. In business it's often all about the wave behind the wave, the bigger opportunity behind the immediate opportunity. Sometimes you have to slow down in order to speed up success.

For example, few companies and brands have received more attention recently than Twitter. The power of a mere 140 characters is literally changing the world. But, few know that Twitter started out as a very different—and unsuccessful—business, Odeo. Initially, their first wave of an idea was to start a company built around making audio text messages and podcasts. But the cost of what was then a new technology and the limits of memory pre-cloud capabilities made it untenable. Eventually, in 2006, Jack Dorsey, Evan Williams, and Biz Stone looked "outside" and shifted their emphasis to text format. Twitter was born. "Twitter grew out of failure," Stone told Oxford University students. "The biggest mistake we made at Odeo was that we were not emotionally invested in the company. We didn't even use podcasts or make podcasts ourselves. Go and build something that you're interested in." Loving what you are doing factors into this, too. Says Stone, "I had a sort of out-of-body experience when I was laughing aloud at something I was working on. That's when it clicked for me that I had this emotional investment that wasn't present with Odeo. It turned out that that would carry me through a lot of hard times; a lot of times when I might otherwise have listened to the naysayers who were saying that Twitter was just a useless toy. Because I was experiencing so much joy, I just kept working."[1]

One of my favorite Big Wave surfer video roundtables was organized in 2012 by Surfline.com.[2] They gathered nine of the best Big Wave surfers for a candid, roundtable discussion about the present status and future possibilities of Big Wave surfing. The video runs about 90 minutes, and at the 17:50 minute mark the topic of preparation comes up.

Laird Hamilton kicks off the discussion by saying he thinks the biggest thing that all Big Wave surfers have in common is that they prepare for a big surf day without knowing when that day will come. Imagine what that is like. Imagine being prepared *in case you need it*. Imagine how hard it is to *wait*.

Laird then adds that a writer once said to him, "It's amazing how patient surfers are." Known as one of the most impatient people in the world, Laird was struck by this comment. Big Wave surfers' lives involve so much waiting. They wait for a set of conditions that might or might not happen, created by Mother Nature's weather pattern arriving at a specific spot with the right swells and winds, and then even when the waves are right they wait their turn in the lineup. That is where dedication meets preparation and preparation meets patience, and every entrepreneur could learn from this.[3]

In one of my conversations with with World Champion Shaun Tomson he added, "It's not like I'm gonna go play golf at 2 p.m. or I'm gonna have a tennis match at 3 p.m. with my mates. I'm looking at the beach and I don't know what I'm gonna get. I'm not gonna be able to control that wave. I'm never gonna be an absolute master of my destiny. It teaches you limits."

I asked, "And patience? Surfing teaches you patience?"

"Surfing teaches you patience and respect for others. There will always be another wave, and all surfers are joined by one ocean. So you don't have to fight to the death for the very next wave," he said. "And sometimes you're in a crowded situation in the lineup and you're getting frustrated, and waves come in sets . . . 6 or 7 of them or 3 or 4 . . . and I have just had to chill. There's gonna be another wave. In business too, there's gonna be another business opportunity. It's not gonna be the same opportunity, it's gonna be another opportunity. So this concept of sitting there and waiting for that opportunity, as a surfer waits for the wave, is pretty profound."

"And always look 'outside,'" I added. "Waves come in sets and there is the wave behind the wave."

"I like that. It has the perspective of having a widespread purpose and looking beyond what's right there in front of you. Like the concept of currents. Different currents. Currents of energy. You never fight a riptide. So there's an awareness in surfers of things stronger than you. You need to humbly accept that and understand it. It's a connectivity with the world. The waves are gonna come to you and build and build and build."[4]

So to always look "outside" has the deeper meaning of *preparation meeting patience*. In business, if you start too soon or let the "exit strategy" overwhelm the "entrance strategy," you give failure unnecessary breathing room.

Preparation and patience are concepts innovators and inventors know well. Father–son co-founders David and Anatole Lokshin created Trace, a device that combines kinetic sensors and GPS technology to track all activity at a given surf session. The action sports tracker first made headlines at San Clemente, California's Trestles beach at the Oakley Lowers Pro 2015.

"Using the data from Trace allows us to look at Lowers in a way that's never been done before," said David Lokshin. "We can look at attributes like speed, take-off points, and board angle to see patterns in the best waves. We use this data to report our findings back to athletes to aid in their strategy."[5]

Much like baseball teams now set their defensive positioning by looking at the "spray charts" that track where a batter tends to hit a ball, Trace tracks the optimal surf break on a given day. With their data, Trace shows where the best surfers gain the most speed and perform the most maneuvers. At The Lowers Pro competition, Trace captured the data of eight surfers.

Lokshin explained that the new venture, funded via Kickstarter, had been in the making his whole life. "As a kid, my dad was always lecturing me about how GPS was going to take over the world," he said. "I woke up in 2010 and realized he was right. We actually left our jobs on the same day without telling each other."

With nine axis sensors, advanced GPS technology, Bluetooth 4.0, and its own processor, Trace is small enough to mount on any board and will track and map your riding time. "Additionally, it will also keep a log of your tricks and rotations, air-time, speed, calories burned, and distance covered. And did we mention it syncs up with your GoPro?"

INVENT THE FUTURE

Pardon the pun, but there is much more "inside" of "outside" than meets the eye, a kind of "zen"-of-the-outside.

Here's what I mean. Let's assume you understand now that there is considerable value in looking at the wave beyond the wave. And let's assume that gathering data has value in surfing, as in business. And let's assume, too, that in the context of work you can readily see the analogy between scanning the horizon and watching for sets of waves in your business or industry. Within the habit of looking "outside" for approaching macro trends, there are microelements to consider too, elements that are so subtle and "deep" they are often missed.

In the *Stoke Report* interview cited earlier, Timothy Leary said, "The danger of the vulgar surfer philosophy is that, 'Oh man, nothing is important; just kick back, wait for the wave, just hang out.' That's beautiful, and it's a step forward, but in a sense it's a dilettante situation. The next step is to create the future, to take responsibility for it."[6]

For the entrepreneur and innovator, how exciting it is to *invent the future* and to feel a responsibility towards that future? So, if you see your work as having a bigger mission than the creation of a new widget or the making of a few bucks, your likelihood of success is considerably higher and your level of satisfaction higher still.

It is the same line of reasoning Steve Jobs had when he was trying to convince John Sculley to leave his job as CEO of Pepsi to come to a then-struggling Apple. At one point, Jobs is said to have told Sculley there was a personal choice to be made: "Do you want to sell sugared water for the rest of your life? Or do you want to come with me and change the world?"[7] Sculley came to Apple.

If nothing else, Steve Jobs was a perfectionist. One trait of all perfectionists is wanting everything to be done "just right." And often this means not rushing to produce something that won't last or have value. Jobs was a master of looking "outside" at customers and markets with patience, even though patience is perhaps the last trait one would associate with Steve Jobs.

The lead designer at Apple throughout the last 20 years of Jobs' life, during introduction of the iPad, and iPhone, was Jony Ive. At Jobs' memorial, which was held on the lawn at Apple's Infinite Loop offices, Ive said, "Steve used to say to me—and he used to say this a lot—'Hey, Jony, here's a dopey idea.' And sometimes they were really dopey. Sometimes they were truly dreadful. But sometimes they took the air from the room, and they left us both completely silent. Bold, crazy, magnificent ideas. Or quiet, simple ones which, in their subtlety, their detail, they were utterly profound."[7] In the ocean, some waves are indeed "dopey," but then conditions change and the "utterly profound" wave comes your way.

Taking a bold idea to fruition, especially for a perfectionist, takes time. When you look "outside," you are seeing the future hurling at you. The best innovators—and Big Wave surfers— do not rush things. Steve Jobs craved products that didn't force adjustments of behavior, products that gave what his wife Laurene Powell Jobs called a "feeling of gratitude that someone else actually thought this through in a way that makes your life easier." She added, "That's what Steve was always looking for . . ."[8]

For example, for the Apple Watch, it was a year before Ive decided on the type of *straps* used to click into slots. Can you imagine the discipline it takes to spend a *year* to determine the right strap for a watch?

On the other hand, the shape of the body of the Apple Watch barely changed from its original concept: a rectangle with rounded corners. Says Ive, "When a huge part of the function is *lists* (of names, dates, or appointments), a circle doesn't make any sense. . . . It's terribly important that you constantly question the assumptions you've made."[9]

TWO-WAVE HOLD-DOWNS

South Africa is known among surfers as " . . . the galling trinity of spectacular waves, cold water, and copious shark encounters. No spot sums this up quite like Dungeons, which sits dormant at the Mouth of Hout Bay in Cape Town."[10]

When winter comes to the Southern Hemisphere, swells build momentum on long stretches of the Southern Atlantic until they pound the reefs across the bay. South African surfer Twig Baker calls it "an awe-inspiring wave for quite a few reasons. Besides the sheer size and power of the wave that makes it so intimidating, it's the location in Hout Bay, surrounded by huge cliffs that plunge to great depths around it and house some of the biggest sharks known to man, that makes it downright terrifying!"[11]

Always looking outside, Twig is smart. He can avoid an idiosyncrasy of many surf spots, the ominous "sneaker sets" of larger waves that seem to come out of nowhere. "When you combine this with the vast, football-size playing field out there it makes it very difficult to surf and means there will always be wide, 'sneaker sets' that catch you off-guard and keep you skittish and on edge. The whole experience leaves you breathless from start to finish."[12]

Surfing *smart* means resisting the "going no matter what" approach. The established Big Wave elite look "outside" and stay smart because they're actually trying to *ride* the oncoming monster waves. That's why on very big days patience and risk aversion kick in, even if it means you leave that day without riding a single wave. At least you literally live to surf another day.

The community of elite Big Wave surfers is still very small, numbering less than 500 men and women worldwide who have ridden waves of 40 feet or more. Most are known and respected by one another if for no other reason than they have all faced the enormity, fury, and power of massive waves. There is an interesting verb in the Big Wave community that is self-explanatory. When slammed by a massive wall of water, surfers will say they got "rag dolled" under water. If twisted, turned, shaken, and jostled when "rag-dolled" you can lose all sense of direction and have to stay mentally calm and focused to avoid drowning.

Then, when you make it to the surface gasping for air, you may face a second wave thundering over you to hold you down a second time. A two-wave hold-down is where the surfer is held under for two consecutive waves and may be unable to get a breath of air in between. This phenomenon is all the more reason to "always look outside," because you will at least know a two-or even three-wave hold-down is a possibility.

At Maverick's, Grant Washburn has learned to look not only "outside," but also "under": "Just beneath the massive peak, a deep hole in the bottom of the ocean inhales seawater, surging violently with each passing swell," he explains. "It's known as 'The Cauldron,' and it's responsible for regular two-wave hold-downs and the deaths of Mark Foo and Sion Milosky. When it is firing on all cylinders [30-foot wave faces or higher], Maverick's provides one of the most feared challenges in sport."[13]

Farther South, in Mexico, Mark Healey describes a massive wipeout at Puerto Escondido. "I made the drop and it kinda half-barreled, which at least let me get in it," Healey said. "Once I pulled in, I saw it run off down the line and jumped off in the barrel. I got obliterated. I was so lucky I had my vest, because there was a three-wave set that came in right after that was bigger. I barely broke the surface with my vest fully inflated. Without vests, there could've been three drownings today. There's not a lot of happy endings out there."[14] Having that vest and looking "outside" to know what was coming, likely saved his life.

Pacific Surf Partners are serial entrepreneurs and early-stage private equity partners that track market trends and align young businesses with those trends. They have rescued many start-ups from harm's way. According to founders George Rubin and Doug Keast, "We view the process of hiring the development and management teams for each individual opportunity as equally important, if not more so. After all, the success of early-stage product development and . . . scale-up depends largely on the people developing the technology." And as surfers themselves, they add metaphorically, "Like the great surfs of the Pacific Ocean, the next market wave can either pass by, crash, or propel one to great heights. The difference is often as simple as timing, [and] we are always ready for the next Big Wave. The difference between riding the crest of the opportunity and sitting in the trough comes down to being in the right place in the right time with some momentum."[15]

LINEUP LOCALISMS

Thus far I have talked about looking "outside" in the spirit of sets and swells and conditions unique to each spot. But there is one further aspect of looking "outside" that has serious business implications—the dreaded human factor.

Many Big Wave surfers live what I call "the endless summer syndrome." In the 1960's, Bruce Brown made a classic surf film with a plot defined by its title, *The Endless Summer*. He films two young surfers as they traipse around the world trying to keep summer alive. The film captured the imagination of the surfing world in part because it fed into every surfer's fantasy: trolling the world, in good company, with no other pressures than finding and surfing good waves.

The popularity of the film led to multiple migrations of surfers heading around the world in search of the "perfect wave."

But there was one major problem: at times the search for perfect surf clashed with local turf. "Local rules," began to surface, which was often not a friendly sight to behold. Another aspect of looking "outside" is to know what the local rules are that guide the lineup, who paddles and when . . . and even whether or not you should lock your car.

For example, Freddy Patacchia was asked about localism on Oahu. What's the best way to go about getting a wave on the North Shore? "In comparison to other spots I've been to around the world, like Northern California or places in Australia and Chile, North Shore isn't that bad. I've paddled out to spots and come in and my rent-a-car has been vandalized. I've gotten yelled at, kicked out of spots, told I couldn't surf there. The thing about Hawaii is everyone can go and paddle out to Pipeline. Everyone. Your car is not going to get vandalized, you're not going to get beat up, you're not going to get told to go in."[16]

That's cool, you may be thinking, but local love only lasts if you know what you are doing and if you play by local rules. "If you get in the way of someone, if you drop in on (cut off) someone, then that's when something happens. So at least in Hawaii you get the benefit of the doubt to a certain extent," he says. "In order to get a wave it's really easy—you sit out in the lineup for about 10 or 15 minutes and observe who the guys are that are sitting at the peak, who is getting all the waves. You can calculate 'Okay, don't drop in on that guy, don't even look at a wave that that guy is looking at' and you can pick off waves that way."[17]

So on any number of levels the failure to look "outside" can have serious consequences, from two-wave hold-downs to breaking unknown local rules in surfing. Knowing the patterns, trends, and habits of the local break has universal benefits.

Looking "outside" includes other subtleties of the local landscape, in the water and on land. Nic Lamb gave me some insights into how different a local community can be depending on which side of the tracks you come from. I knew he grew up for many years in Santa Cruz, CA, and that he knew Jay Moriarity, so I asked, "Was there a connection via Santa Cruz that you had with Jay Moriarity?"

47

"I don't know if you know a lot about Santa Cruz, but there is that West side/East side thing. I was raised on the West side and the West side was a bit more aggressive. And the guys I grew up with were like doing heavy drugs, the Rolling Stones of surfers. Really gnarly, aggressive guys. So in turn I had to build like a tough exterior to protect myself. And as you get older, you realize it's all bullshit, 'cause people in the real world are nice. I'm 27 now and it's like from 12–17 these guys were mean, like really fucking mean. They'd make you cry and beat the shit out of you. But Jay, on the East side . . . the elders there were a little more professional, a little bit more friendly and, like, sweet. So that's the product . . . you get Jay. [On the other hand there's] Flea and those guys from on the West side, just 10 miles away."[18]

So there are many layers to looking "outside," from water conditions to local rules that affect your chances in the water. The same is true in business.

David Butler is the Vice President of Innovation for Coca-Cola. He also learned a lot about business from surfing. "I grew up surfing. Even if the closest you've ever come to surfing is watching *The Endless Summer* or *Blue Crush* with a bag of popcorn, you probably understand that surfing is all about being in the right place at the right time."

Echoing The Surfer's Rules, he says, "Of course, you need to know how to swim, have a board, and know a little bit about how tides work. But the real skill is being able to look out into the horizon and see the sets or patterns of waves building, then position yourself to make the most of them."

Butler knows that surfers and entrepreneurs have much to share. As he puts it, "They're both constantly searching for the next Big Wave. Being able to identify patterns and make the most of them is critical when trying to start a company or keep the one you have growing. I think the next wave of innovation and entrepreneurship is building; you can see it on the horizon. However, we all have to be in the right position—as individuals, as well as companies—if we want to catch it. So let's look to a future where entrepreneurship and design are democratized and available to everyone."[19]

When I talked to Jeff Clark, he described how he and Jay Moriarity prepared in macro ways to be in the right place at the right time for Big Waves: "You gotta give yourself the *overall* picture of success, and that's taking into account every condition. What's the surface of the first wave? What's the surface of the second wave? Third and fourth? And pick your best opportunity for success. I think sometimes adrenaline overrides good thinking. And that's when you have problems.

"I had a tow partner at a Jaws event. And the way he prepares for something and the way I prepare for something are very different. I go 'inside' (myself), I fortify inside-out, not outside-in. Outside-in doesn't work. [On the other hand] . . . I think a lot of people prepare with a gung ho attitude. And you can do that. You can get strong. And you can hold your breath for five minutes. But if your mind won't let you make that right decision at the right time it's not gonna help you. It's really important to be calm in big surf . . . nervous energy will get you killed."

For example, Jeff told me a story of one instance of being calm in the midst of a storm. "Jay Moriarity was my tow partner at Maverick's and my gosh, one day I let go of the rope too soon while we were messing around on the lefts, and all of a sudden I'm hip-hoppin' and trying to get down the wave face, and that ledge comes out underneath me and I pull out the back and the wave just *unloads*. And there's a bigger one right behind it," he says.

"And Jay comes rolling in (on a Jet Ski), he slides the (attached safety) sled up to me, and I had fallen and my booties

49

get stuck in my straps, and I'm upside down in the water, and I come up and the sled's right there, and I throw my board on and Jay goes 'what are you doing?', and he's laughin' and then he says 'we gotta go!' And I didn't even say anything. He is gonna take care of the ski, because if he gets taken out with the ski, then we're both swimming in from out there," he says. "And I just barely get myself on the sled and the next wave is like 30 feet and just looming over us and we're in its shadow and it's dark and . . . Jay just rode the left out! We were probably in the barrel . . . with the ski! And that kind of calm under pressure is what made Jay who he was and why we got along so well. We knew the parameters of the equipment we were using, and the place we were playing. We knew how to play in our sandbox. And we could take it to the very edge knowing we could dance with that kind of power. And be calm. And that's what makes it so fun."[20]

STRATEGY WINS

As we have seen, being calm in the face of danger is just one trait of the Big Wave surfers. Calm is cool, but when pro surfers are in competitions on the world tour, there is another factor that is often missed—the importance of *strategy*. Nearly every businessperson will have some kind of a strategic plan, and the same holds for Big Wave surfers. Former world champion Barton Lynch recently spoke on the importance of strategy during competitions. While criticizing the on-air commentary of surf announcers he said, "I have never watched a heat and felt as if it's been properly explained how and why someone lost or won. Occasionally a surfer will come in and tell you that he lost the heat because he misused 'priority' [who goes first] here, or did something else wrong there, and you get some insight into what actually went down. Kelly [Slater] is great at this."

Then Lynch hit the nail on the head: "Most commentators don't like the fact that every heat is actually won by wave selection, the use of priority, and the management of time—by strategy, basically. Commentators almost deny the existence of strategy and try and make us believe heats are won by just surfing. My experience is that heats are less often won by surfing, and more often won by strategy, and this is what actually makes it interesting."[21]

It is not all fun and games when those huge swells roll in. And in business, too often the entrepreneur is oblivious to the role of strategy. Yet the presence of a good strategy will ultimately determine what will succeed and what won't. Strategy is to business as what looking "outside" is to surfing: it tells you what is coming, where to position yourself, and, as the next chapter will tell you, when it's time to commit, charge, and shred.

SURFER STEP
4

ALWAYS LOOK "OUTSIDE"

Surfers have long periods in the water while waiting their turn in the lineup for the wave they want. As waves build, they come in sets. The sets do not produce identical waves, so surfers always look "outside" at the waves behind the wave and/or at the sets in the far distance. This way, they can better select a wave, be in the right position at the right time, and enhance their chances of success.

Entrepreneurs are no different. It is not only important they know what is happening right now regarding a product or

51

ALWAYS LOOK "OUTSIDE"

service, but they should also understand what is coming on the horizon. Many entrepreneurs fail because they develop an idea or product based solely on what is or was, only to launch their product and find out a competitor has a better product they were unaware of.

For example, Ocean Spray is a typical consumer packaged goods company, with one unique element. It is owned by a farmer's cooperative, but run by seasoned industry professionals. One of them, Chief Operating Officer, Ken Romanzi, had never seen a cranberry harvest but was finally persuaded by someone in the grower relations department to take a look. Then, he finally did. "It took my breath away," he says. Up to that point he had only looked at "the numbers," the proverbial low hanging fruit (pun intended). His vision was myopic. He had never looked "outside," but when he did he had a revelation. "This is nature's most beautiful harvest. There's gotta be a way we can get this in front of consumers." This was the birth of the idea of filming cranberry bogs around the world and then featuring them in a very successful advertising campaign—a tactic that made Ocean Spray number one in its category.[22]

For the innovator, to look "outside" is more than the trite notion of "outside the box." "Outside" in this context means *way* outside—seeing things anew by having fresh eyes, and transforming pre-existing ideas by simplifying them. So for the innovator, trusting in serendipity or juxtaposition—or a cranberry bog—can be the key.

With all the preparation of mind, body, and spirit in place, it is time to "Put your head down, and *paddle!*" We are nearly halfway through this book, and with all the prior steps described in the previous chapters in place, only now are we finally ready ride! It took a while, but it's worth the wait.

As the Big Wave surfers say, it's time to "Commit, Charge, Shred!"

THINGS TO DO:

Too often entrepreneurs become myopic. So enamored with their own ideas, they fail to see what other options are out there. Ask yourself these key questions to stave off this tunnel vision:

1. What business trends do you see that match well with your product or service? List those trends then articulate specifically how/why there is a match.

2. Who are your competitors and what are they up to? Which of those competitors might make a good strategic *partner* in the future?

3. What direct feedback have you gathered from your customers? How has this feedback affected the iterations of your idea?

4. What human, technological, and material resources are still missing?

With your answers to Questions 1-4 in mind, are you ready to launch?

Write down your answers and do nothing with them for 48 hours. Patience will pay off. After the wait, read what you have written and reduce each answer to no more than three brief sentences. Finally, pretend you are going to read your remarks to fifth graders and edit out any sentences that contain business jargon. The challenge here is to keep your plan clear and simple . . . and less than a page long.

Armed with your one-pager, answer the questions posed in the "To, By, For" process as follows:

- TO do what? What is the basic plan/idea?
- BY whom, BY when? (Who will execute what parts of the plan, and by when?)
- FOR what purpose? (Why are you doing each aspect of the plan? What are the desired outcomes of each phase of the plan?)

5

COMMIT, CHARGE, SHRED!

I N EVERY SPORT THERE ARE MANY SUPERSTARS, A FEW CHAM-
pions, and an occasional iconic legend. In surfing there are only
a few legends on whom almost everyone can agree: Duke
Kahanamoku, Eddie Aikau, Miki Dora, Shaun Tomson, Clyde
Aikau, Tom Carroll, Tom Curren, Laird Hamilton, and Kelly
Slater are 9 of my top 10. The tenth, to me, is the late Andy Irons.

Some in the surfing world may not agree with me, and in
terms of full disclosure I admit that I am a bit biased. Hanalei,
Kauai—Andy's birthplace—holds a special place in my life. I
first went to Hanalei in the early 1970s. I later honeymooned
there, and with my family subsequently spent more than two-
dozen summers just north of Pine Trees. My five kids all learned
to swim and surf on the north end of Hanalei Bay where Weke
Road ends. I remember watching Andy Irons and his brother
Bruce train, swim, and surf from when they were young teens.

Andy's mom worked at the Hanalei surf shop, and my blue-collar family of seven would parade in to get supplies and grab a shave ice nearby.

In a video tribute posted recently on his birthday, Andy talked about his first wave.

"The first wave I ever caught I remember to this day, clear as day. I went left, right, left [in the barrel or tube of the wave], and the wave never broke. And I thought right then this is the coolest thing in the world! And from that day on I told my mom every night, 'I wanna go surfing I wanna go surfing I wanna go surfing,'" he says. "It all started with goin' left-right-left with one wave at the pier. I literally will never forget that wave. To the day I die that was like one of the most purest moments of my whole life and it always will be."[1]

As in starting any enterprise, the first experience often shapes all future endeavors. And in business, so much of one's success depends on the preparation and hard work that preceded the launch. Most small businesses and entrepreneurial endeavors fail, in large part due to lack of patience and preparation. Here again, the lessons to be learned from Big Wave surfers come to the fore—there comes a time when you commit, when you know the time is now, when you just swing the board around, put your head down, and *paddle*!

"It's all about the feeling I get from riding that wave," says Andy Irons. "That first wave is the reason why everyone keeps coming back. It's like anything. If you didn't like it, you're not gonna go back and do it again. Like I tried ice-skating I hated it. I didn't go back again ever . . . Surfing, if you catch a good wave, you're hooked! Right then and there."

When you tackle Big Waves you have a number of "first waves," one for each big day at a new Big Wave surf spot. Reflecting in a video interview on his first ride at Teahupo'o, Irons says, "Any wave I think back to, there's no wave that sticks out more than the one at Teahupo'o . . . I was frozen with fear. Like I thought I was gonna die . . . Before that wave came through I told Mark Healey . . . 'I can't catch a wave, I won't even go. I'm like, every wave is 15 foot and *dredging* and I've pulled back on five waves and my balls are just up in my stomach, I'm patching, I'm scared, I can't do it.' And [Healey's] like, 'Don't worry, just get over the ledge, get over the ledge.' I remember Healey told me straight, 'Get over the ledge on the next one and I guarantee it'll be a turning point.' And that was the wave. And it literally was a turning point to my whole life."[2]

Even Mark Healey, his mentor, has his moments too—times when he has to follow his own advice. The enormous surf that batters south-facing beaches in Mexico and California is fed by storms from the Southern Hemisphere. With modern forecasting tools, Big Wave surfers know up to a week in advance where in the world the next major Big Wave sets are heading.

Once, Healey, an XL pro surfer with lots of experience in Hawaii's big surf flew to Mexico to greet the swell in Puerto Escondido. There, waves were so large and thunderous with water that the beach shook when they crashed on the shore. Watching from the shore, even the best of surfers thought twice about paddling out. "It was twice as big as I've ever seen Puerto," Healey told *Surfline*. "I made the 30-minute paddle from the harbor, and within 15 minutes this wave came in."

Looking "outside," Healey said, " . . . when you're paddling and it's huge, you know . . . 40, 50 foot faces you first see the swell on the horizon in a set. You can see miles out to sea when it's that big. You can see the swells coming, and you've got some time . . . and people start getting nervous . . . the few guys that stay inside are running a huge risk . . . so it really comes down to—and this part I really love—it's holding your ground . . . even when it looks like one of those movie tidal wave scenes.

"It doesn't seem right, and even for me every instinct in your body is saying 'run!' You have to force yourself to be there . . . at some point I make up my mind no matter what happens, I'm goin'," he said. "It's gonna be a very thin line between making it and not making it. You don't always know where that line is until you just try it. The biggest waves I've ever ridden, none of them seemed makeable when I was paddling for it . . . I know you've just really gotta commit . . .

"I made the drop and it kinda half-barreled, which at least let me get in it," Healey recalled. "Once I pulled in, I saw it run off down the line and jumped off in the barrel. I got obliterated. I was so lucky I had my vest, because there was a three-wave set that came in right after that that was bigger."[3]

TURN AND CHARGE!

Reflecting the entrepreneurial spirit, Big Wave surfer Ken Bradshaw says, "I really enjoy big waves. It's truly a test of your ability to surf. It takes passion. It takes desire to make yourself go over that ledge, to risk everything to catch that wave."[4]

In an article on entrepreneurs who surf, Nicholas Mohnacky, CEO of Surfr App, which connects surfers with surfing spots, shops, food, and lodging says, "In surfing, you have the option to sit on the shoulder or sit on the peak of the wave. When that set wave approaches, it can be intimidating because you know you're in the right spot and your friends are hooting at you to go. As the wave approaches, you only have two options: paddle over the top or turn and charge."

Extending that moment to business he says, "Entrepreneurship requires you to charge. There's no paddling over the sets or sitting on the shoulder. You have to go for the set wave, peer over the ledge, paddle in, pick a line, put your head down, and take off. Really, up until that moment when you decide to paddle in, you're just a spectator," he says. "In the same way surfers train and prepare their bodies for all that the ocean can throw at them, entrepreneurs must be ready to persevere and overcome the turmoil of fund raising, sales, development issues, creative stalemates and communication problems."[5]

PUT YOUR HEAD DOWN AND PADDLE!

Bianca Valenti is a Northern Californian surfer who has surfed some of the biggest waves in the world. With her father, she is also involved in a very successful restaurant and has learned a lot about business from her professional surfing, especially regarding the special challenges waterwomen face. Via women's XL surfing groups like Super Sessions, she is an ambassador for more equality in surfing in general and on the professional Big Wave circuit specifically. She recently talked about the reactions to women in the lineup when the Big Waves are happening. "People see men charging Big Waves, and they think 'Oh, those guys are nuts.' Then they see women surf Big Waves, and their minds bend," she says.

"I got all the Hawaiian girls who were with me to surf a big Maverick's day . . . and they all caught waves. I think that was a real eye-opener for [the guys], for everybody. We knew it was going to be crowded, and we knew the swell was on the increase, so we started out just watching the cam at my house; then we all went down to the cliff to look at it, then finally I just said 'We're getting our wetsuits on now.'

"I sort of forced us all to go out. A few of the Hawaiians were like, 'If I catch one wave, I'm going in.' But then Keala [Kennelly] got a good one, and she was so stoked, and [she] paddled back out. Paige Alms got a few bombs. Andrea Möller got some too."

Just as in surfing, you establish a track record of success in business when you prove yourself in the marketplace. In the water that day, the respect was coming from all the guys in the lineup. The women showed their skill and their will. "They're super-nice to almost everyone out there. At the same time, you have to prove yourself." Then she adds, "Nobody's going to say 'It's your turn, go.' If you want the wave and you're the one in position, the only way you're going to get it is if you put your head down and paddle."[6]

In surfing and business, attitude and confidence count. At only 30 years old, Sophia Amoruso became one of the most influential figures in retail and a cultural icon who worked from the ground up. Amoruso's Nasty Gal first sparked a cult following as a one-woman vintage clothing venture on eBay, where her fearless eye for fashion and outrageous style enabled her to "translate 'likes' into sales." In just five years (and after being kicked off eBay), the brand grew into a one-stop shop and online retail haven with a progressive following of fashion risk-takers and well over a hundred million dollars in revenue. She went all-in and never held back.

To be "all in" means overcoming lifelong fears. As Greg Long says, "I do feel fear. But that fear is one of the underlying motivators of why I ride big waves. How are we ever meant to truly grow in our lives if we don't occasionally step out of that comfort zone? The feelings of fear, I open my arms and I welcome them."

Reflecting on a 40-foot wave at Cortes Bank, "I turn around, put my head down and paddle my heart out. I would have rather gone on that wave and eaten shit and wiped out, than sat there for the rest of my life and wondered could I have made it? I paddled back out and I wanted to do it again . . . I wanted to make one of these waves."[7] Greg Long will have no regrets about Cortes Bank because he faced his fear.

I asked Shaun Tomson if he remembered his first big wave. Without hesitation he said, "It was 1969 in Makaha and I was 14 years old. It was the biggest swell of 1969 and supposedly the biggest swell in years. And I was there on a bar mitzvah trip. There was only one break on the whole of the North Shore that was rideable, and it was Makaha. We were driving around the island looking. Waimea Bay was just this huge lip. So we drove back to Makaha, because we were staying in Makaha. Because it was so bad, there was a very long period between swells. So we drove up. It's a beautiful day. December in Hawaii. The coast looked so inviting so I just grabbed my board and paddled out," he says. "Paddled all the way out, maybe half a mile. And there's a group of maybe six guys, all the best surfers in the world and they look at me and they say, 'what are you doing out here?' Then these mountains start coming in. Mountains!"

I asked, "Who would that group have been . . . Eddie Aikau and those guys?"

"No. Greg Noll. Randy Rarick, Keith Paull, Rolf Aurness . . . But everyone's on their own. And it's interesting; it's not unlike business. Ultimately you're on your own. No one's holding your hand. Sure, if you get into trouble, surfers will be there for you. There's commonality, camaraderie," he said. "Especially when that big set comes and when that Big Wave comes, that huge wave. When you swing around, no one's telling you to go or telling you not to go. That decision, that spark inside you that pushes you over the edge, it's yours and yours alone. It's actually a process I've found of breaking through that fear barrier, because everyone has fears."[8]

On the *Stoke* Report, Timothy Leary said, "One thing I like about surfing is that it is all out. You can't be half-hearted, or you can't be thinking about something else. You've got to give

61

up all the land, social, cultural, moral, political whatevers . . . you've got to be totally there." He adds, "And I think . . . well, that's my approach to life. I'm only interested in people who are willing to go and do it."[9]

Consider Professor Sarah Gerhardt, who shocked the world when she became the first woman to surf Maverick's in 1999. The wife of Big Wave surfer Mike Gerhardt, Sarah has been a fixture at Maverick's ever since. In addition to holding a PhD in physical chemistry and being a college professor in Santa Cruz, CA, Sarah is one of the most respected big wave riders, and she never misses a big swell at Maverick's.

Her approach and preparation are quite analytical and focused. "I don't know the chemistry of the brain. I do have quite a bit of experience using my mind and breath to control the central nervous system's response to big waves, however."

As with all Big Wave surfers, knowing the lead-time before a big swell is predicted to arrive helps her to prepare for her surfing—and her family, as well. "There is a lot of planning, with my husband, on how to coordinate work and children since we both surf out there," she said. "Then when the day arrives, and adrenaline starts pumping the minute we are in the truck on the way up the coast. I usually try to remain tranquil and absorb all of the beauty of the coast . . ." she says.

After arriving at the spot and getting into her wetsuit comes "paddling for 20 to 45 minutes to make it out to the lineup. I catch my breath and marvel at the waves and their riders, trying to psych myself up to catch some for myself," she says. "It takes patience and persistence to remain in the perfect location for catching a wave, and after all that, sometimes the adrenaline is too much and I look down 30 or more feet and stop paddling. When I can override my survivor instinct and huck myself over the ledge of a wave, then it's just the sheer thrill of speed.

"The elation of successfully riding a wave is indescribable. I can only relate it to the feeling we all have experienced of accomplishing a task that was deemed impossible."[10]

Like the Big Wave surfers, the best entrepreneurs know that you have to go all out to be all-in.

Similarly, Greg Long adds, "The ocean is this amazing metaphor for life, if you think about it. You are on this constantly moving playing field. You know the winds, tides, currents are always changing. Tides go in, out, there's ebb and a flow to everything," he says.[11]

During our conversation Shaun Tomson described the aesthetic pleasures that come after you commit to the wave. "Many surfers will tell you that at certain times in the tube, at critical high speeds, they experience the sensation of the wave moving in slow motion. The body is reacting to danger. When you cannot fight, and you cannot run, the senses go to red alert where every nerve becomes a seismograph, registering and reacting to the slightest shift in the immediate environment." Then he added, "In this altered, hypersensitive state of mind and body, the wave actually appears to churn in slow motion. The result is that you feel like you have all the time in the world to react."[12]

On facing a big wave for the first time at Bonzai Pipeline, Tomson says he had his doubts for a split second. "I was in this moment of hesitation, and I put my head down with absolute commitment. And that single wave changed my life because once I made the commitment, . . . once I knew I was gonna go over that edge, . . . all the fear went away. It's incredible. The commitment takes the fear away."[13]

Cape Town, South Africa, surfer Matt Bromley also recalls how going to that edge and then over it takes the fear away. Describing how he attempted to paddle into one of the biggest waves ever recorded, he says "You think about that one wave . . . the one that's right at the edge of your limits and challenges all of your life's preparation . . . That's what this one felt like. Alex Gray had just caught a quick one and snapped his leash, so I was left hanging way out the back dodging massive sets. I was terrified and suddenly my chunky [surfboard] felt tiny!" Undaunted, he looked outside. "Then this set popped up. I missed the first one, but paddling for it positioned me a little bit further in. The next wave came in, and I was faced with one of the craziest chunks of water I've ever seen. I thought to myself, *This is it. Here we go.* So I put my head down and paddled like crazy."[14]

IT'S NOT ABOUT THE SIZE OF THE WAVE

Ryan Seelbach, San Francisco-based geologist and Big Wave surfer, tells a similar story. "I enjoy getting scared, the adrenaline of the occasional wipeout . . . getting stuck in certain situations. I get scared like everybody else, but I just kinda deal with it." To accommodate his surfing passion, he negotiated with his boss to take some time off and work a 30-hour schedule. "I took a pay cut so I could surf more. But it's worth it."

At the 2013 The Maverick's Surf Competition, Seelbach was competing while nursing bruised ribs from an earlier wipeout. "So when I jumped on my board and paddled out . . . I was like 'I don't know how long I can do this for' . . . and I saw a wave, a set coming, and I paddled over into position and I was like 'I'm going,' and I just committed to it way early and I just put my head down and paddled as hard as I could."

Not over-thinking and trusting his preparation, training, and instincts, he knew it was time to make his move. "I try not to focus on the size of the wave when I'm going for 'em. I just see it and just try and go. I always realize, looking back, 'that was a Big Wave.'"[15]

Similarly, fellow Maverick's competitor Alex Martins says, "When you start the paddle out, every day is a different day out there . . . You're gonna get bombed, you know. But we're not crazy people. We prepare ourselves for this," he says. "One day I got the biggest wave of my life. I paddled as hard as I could and I thought I had the wave for a second. But I felt my board hit this speed bump or something. I pretty much lost control. I felt like 'Oh my god! This is it!' If you play with fire you're gonna get burned at some point . . . There was at the beginning of the heat a huge one, and I'm like, I'm not even gonna look. I'm just gonna swing and go! . . . For me it was a dream come true. I had the day of my life."[16]

With Big Waves, as with business, you have to be committed. There comes a moment when there is no turning back. Everything, *everything* is facing "forward." Nothing behind you matters at that moment. Nerves of steel are not enough; you need nerves of titanium. Every entrepreneur craves that moment when all preparation has readied you for the launch, even though success is not guaranteed.

BELIEVE HARD

I repeat: New businesses fail 9 out of 10 times. The numbers are not that high in Big Wave surfing, but when there is a wipeout, it can be horrendous. Even so, falling is part of riding, and serious wipeouts are part of the Big Wave sport.

Few wipeouts generated more heated debate than that of Maya Gabeira in 2013 at Nazaré, Portugal. For starters, questions were raised as to whether she should have been out at all in *80-foot* conditions. Then came questions about a Jet Ski tow-in vs. paddling in. Recently, the world's top Big Wave surfers have moved away from towing and back to paddling in.

Hawaiian Dave Wassell summed it up at the Billabong XXL awards, saying, "Big Waves are meant to paddle. You aren't born with a Jet Ski."[17] While Gabeira does paddle into Big Waves, most of her notoriety has come from her tow-in surfing prowess. Regarding her preference for tow-in surfing to paddling, she said with a laugh "I really got it all wrong when I was born."

That day at Nazaré, she did head out on a high-speed Jet Ski with her mentor, 2002 World Champion Big Wave surfer Carlos Burlé driving, to face some of the biggest waves ever attempted. She watched a few swells, then saw a large set moving in. She got into the water before Carlos and was towed into a massive wall of water. She stayed up on her board quite a while as it bounced hard three or four times before she was overtaken by a huge wall of foam and water and rag-dolled into a massive wipeout. A second wave soon arrived, and Maya was in trouble. Video footage shows her surfacing, head bobbing, as another wave pounds her. She then resurfaces, floating facedown in the water. At this point, Carlos realizes he must risk everything and he races in with the Jet Ski and drags her onto the beach. On the shore, CPR begins and she is revived, saved from death's door. Only after she is rushed to the hospital does she find out that she has also broken her ankle.

The severity of her accident was not unusual in the Big Wave community. "In 2010, former World Tour surfer Shane Dorian nearly drowned during a two-wave hold-down at Maverick's in Northern California. Dorian was so rattled after the experience that he considered retiring," reported Matt Skenazy.

"In 2012, Greg Long fell at Cortes Bank, a surf spot 100 miles off the coast of Los Angeles and was held under until he blacked out. After being pulled to the surface, he had to be airlifted to the hospital," wrote Skenazy. "While both incidents garnered considerable attention in the surf world, neither Long's nor Dorian's actions or skills were ever called into question. This isn't a surprise—they're two of the top Big-Wave surfers on the planet. But," he adds, "dozens of other male surfers, many of whom have less experience and training than Gabeira, have died, nearly died, or seriously injured themselves while surfing big waves, without receiving any condemnation."[18]

Well-known surfers like Laird Hamilton were very critical of Maya and Carlos. After Gabeira's wipeout video was viewed by nearly 10 million people, it seemed as though everyone had an opinion. Said one commentator, "The Internet is aflutter with people questioning her ability. It's a sexist question. The fact that Maya is female seems to have made everyone uncomfortable."[19]

But she was riled up and taking on her critics soon after the accident. "I think Laird's words have an air of prejudice, of machismo," she told a reporter a week after the wipeout. "He doesn't want to believe. He doesn't want to see a young girl in this position, having this kind of exposure surfing huge waves."[20]

Keala Kennelly, another woman with the skills and sponsors to chase large waves, somewhat disagreed with Maya. "They would have said the same statements had the surfer in question been male," said Kennelly, who grew up on Kauai and was mentored by Hamilton. "If women are going to be taken seriously and respected alongside the male big-wave-surfing greats, then we should be held to similar performance standards."[21]

But whether a Big Wave surfer is male or female, rich or poor, young or old, . . . the ocean always wins—much in the same way that the marketplace always determines what it wants and what it doesn't.

"Maverick's is a spot that takes care of itself . . . When that set comes, your heart starts to pound, and when you take off every ounce of adrenaline in your body is pumping. It sounds like

COMMIT, CHARGE, SHRED!

thunder when the wave crashes," says Jeff Clark. "You have to be 100% committed to ride Big Waves."[22] Says Maverick's regular Ryan Seelbach, "Every time I go out (to Maverick's) it's special."[23]

In a short film on Andy Irons called *I Surf Because* . . . , released to commemorate his birthday, Andy talked about the importance the ocean played in his life. "I have a lot of inner demons. If I didn't have surfing, I'd self-destruct . . . without it I'd tip into oblivion . . . I surf because I'm always a better person when I come in."[24]

To the Big Wave surfer, the reward-to-risk ratio always tips in the direction of the rewards. As Evan Slater says, "People are like, 'Well, what about a wipeout?' Well that's almost more fun than a successful ride 'cause you *really* test yourself. I personally think there's just a certain personality type who feels a little bit of regret or feels anxiety if they're *not* at the biggest spot on any given day or getting the most out of a large swell or a Big Wave . . . That's the feeling that you're always chasing."[25]

As Timothy Leary said on *Stoke Report*, "I've picked out as my symbol (of life), surf; and I want to have film of a surfer right at that point moving along constantly right at the edge of the tube. That position is the metaphor of life to me, the highly conscious life." And why is it that putting your head down and paddling is a metaphor for the highly conscious life? " . . . You think of the tube as being the past . . . that point where you're going into the future, but you have to keep in touch with the past . . . There's where you get the power . . . and sure you're most helpless, but you also have most precise control at that moment."[26]

With similar exuberance, Mason Ho succinctly describes that precise moment coming out of the tube of the wave: " . . . BOOM! [When I] come out of the barrel . . . I want my pants to be over my head!"[27] That's what it means to commit, charge, and shred.

COMMIT, CHARGE, SHRED!

When you choose the wave you want, it is time to "commit." As the late Jay Moriarity used to say, "Don't hesitate." To "catch" a wave you have to be moving faster than the speed of the wave. Waves can move at speeds in excess of 40 miles per hour. So, you have to start to paddle early and get up enough speed to "drop in," to ride. This requires being in the right position at the right time combined with the courage to go for it!

For entrepreneurs, staying ahead of the wave has clear applications. Optimizing your chances requires making a commitment, staying focused on the endeavor, and working hard well in advance of the "launch." At that point, everyone has to be ready to roll—with no hesitation, at a moment's notice.

That's why Sun Microsystems CEO and Founder Scott McNealy was fond of saying you should have "all the wood behind one arrowhead." It's also why for an April Fools' Day prank one year his employees snuck into his office and placed a huge telephone pole that extended out of his window. At one end of the pole was an arrowhead, on the other some makeshift feathers! Ever the good sport, McNealy had a good laugh and wore a mock arrow headgear that day. The photo of this is priceless.[28]

Innovators by definition are ahead of the wave. They make their mark by being the first to market with a new product or service before the competitors can see it coming. As I teach in my Innovating for Results™ training programs, by using a number of unconventional tools—like . . . tracking customers'

69

"mis-uses and abuses" of a product . . .—they gain a competitive advantage. Still, all this planning and preparation and hard work do not guarantee success at the launch. It may be necessary to iterate, revise, and stay flexible and resilient, making agility your new best friend. Even the greatest Big Wave surfers fall daily, but as we will see in the next chapter, they learn from each fall and paddle back out.

THINGS TO DO:

The launch is imminent. You have done your homework well. You have created a plan based on what you know about your customers, the competition, and the marketplace. You have gathered the necessary human, technological, and material resources. Now it is time to execute. There is no turning back.

This is the moment you have waited and planned for. But much like a Big Wave surfer has to make instantaneous adjustments to the delightful reality of a given wave, you must also be prepared to adjust in real time. Ask yourself these questions:

1. How will I monitor and track the first days, weeks, and months after the launch?

2. What milestones am I looking for the first days, weeks, and months?

3. By whom, by what process, and by when will decisions be made to make adjustments and corrections in real time following the launch? Be very specific.

6
PADDLE
BACK OUT

WHO KNEW MARK TWAIN WAS . . . A SURFER? IN HIS JOUR-
nal from June 1907, he wrote, "I got the board placed
right, and at the right moment, too, but missed the connection
myself. The board struck the shore in three quarters of a second,
without any cargo, and I struck the bottom about the same
time, with a couple of barrels of water in me."[1] Another famous
writer surfed too . . . Jack London. In an article entitled "Riding
the South Seas Surf," the adventurer wrote about visiting friends
in Waikiki and of his first encounter with riding ocean waves.
"I tried for a solid hour and not one wave could I persuade to
boost me forward."[2] A good swimmer, he sat, listened and
watched the waves being ridden by a local Kanaka, " . . . a man,
a natural king, a member of the kingly species . . ." *That* is what
it is: a royal sport for the natural kings of earth."[3]

  "It is all very well, sitting here in the cool shade of the beach,"
he told himself, "but you are a man, one of the kingly species,

71

and what that Kanaka can do you can do yourself . . . Get in and wrestle with the sea; wing your heels with the skill and power that reside in you; bite the sea's breakers, master them, and ride upon their backs as a king should."[4]

With that self-encouragement, he talked himself into the ocean to try again to surf.

Having psyched himself up, he grabbed a small wood board and headed into the water, where he again realized that he was a much better writer than surfer! He tried to copy the Kanaka—laying on the board, kicking, paddling, and standing up as they did. "The breaker swept past, and I was not on it." He was, in his own words, an "ignominious failure."

Finally, his friend Alexander Hume Ford, who had been surfing for about a month, stepped in. "Look at the way you're trying to ride it. If ever the nose of that board hits bottom, you'll be disembowelled. Here," Ford said, "Take my board. It's a man's size."[5]

Just as happens to many of us early on in our quest to learn to surf, London was given a surfing lesson by a friend. Ford showed him where to position himself on the board, how to lay prone, and how to time his paddle after looking "outside." All of this preceded a good shove of the board from Ford that helped him catch up to his first wave. "Ah," said London, a "delicious moment when I felt that breaker grip and fling me!" Now he was hooked; he was stoked! In an hour or so, he was beginning to get rides. Even so, on occasion "that miserable board poked its nose down to bottom, stopped abruptly, and turned a somersault, at the same time violently severing our relations."[6] To his credit, London persisted. He now understood this chapter's theme: if you fall, learn from it and go back out again.

Fast-forward three decades to much bigger waves and very experienced surfers with the same initial results faced by Mark

Twain and Jack London. "The pioneers of big wave surfing started to eye impossible killer rides in the 1940's," according to surfertoday.com. "In the 1960's, waves like Pipeline and Waimea increased the popularity of paddling into new wave heights. Going over the falls was the daily menu."[7]

YOU GOTTA PAY TO PLAY

The world of work today is changing so often and so quickly that those with a surfer's mindset are at a distinct advantage. If you *prepare* for falls and see falling as a learning experience, you are a step ahead of everyone else. The value of perseverance and going back into the fray after the fall are intrinsic to the entrepreneur's world, too. For the innovator, failure affords a new starting point. Given the failure rate of ideas, businesses, and start-ups, adopting the surfer's mindset of "fall, learn, paddle back out" becomes a competitive advantage.

According to a recent *Forbes* article by Neil Patel, "Nine out of ten start-ups fail. This is a hard and bleak truth, but one that you'll do well to meditate on. Entrepreneurs may even want to write their failure post-mortem before they launch their business. Why? Because every optimistic entrepreneur needs a dose now and then," he says. "It's all about recovering from blows. Teams that are able to recover together also possess the unique trait of harmoniously working together through tough times."[8]

Mick Ebeling, founder of Not Impossible Labs, says, "When you hit a major obstacle, you've just got to think 'Well that's not an option anymore . . . what else *can* I do?'"[9] "Like nothing else," says surfer/entrepreneur Ben Martin, creator of the Johnny on the Spot surf app, "when you first start out (surfing) you're gonna try, try, and try and fail, fail, and fail. Cold water will rush through your sinuses. Your arms will feel like someone's

73

tried to rip them from your body. People will shout at you telling you to get out of their way. And yet, you can see those guys just beyond the breakers gliding along the face of the waves like they were raised by a pod of dolphins. Don't let the failure hurt you. Get back on your board, stick with it, and you'll get there. Once again—sound familiar? . . . maybe [to] business?"[10]

As *Surfer* magazine says, "You gotta pay to play, it's an adage that's especially true for surfers. As soon as you start surfing you'll find yourself with fin gashes, leash burns, lumps, bruises, and beat downs on the regular."[11] You learn to ride by learning to roll with what the waves throw at you.

So, the reality is that falling happens, for surfers and for entrepreneurs. The pioneers of Big Wave surfing knew that going over the falls every session was the rule, not the exception. So facing their fears was a given.

Fear is one way of "managing the risk of paddling for a huge wave face, which doesn't tell you what is going to happen and how it is going to break," says *Surfer Today* magazine.[12]

"Big Wave surfers are not interested in performance," says Jordy Lawler. "Forget perfect cutbacks, stunning floaters, or breathless aerial antics . . . Monster waves tend to move quickly and force surfers to get away from the powerful whitewater. Big Waves are lethal even for the most experienced extreme riders. The best Big Wave surf spots in the world have claimed several lives in the last decades."[13]

The death of a seasoned Big Wave surfer is sobering, and fortunately quite rare. Surfers like Malik Joyeux and Japanese surfer Moto Watanabe (Jaws/Pipeline), Sion Milosky and the legendary Mark Foo (Maverick's), Donnie Solomon (Waimea Bay), Todd Chesser (Outside Alligator Rock, Oahu), Dickie Cross (Waimea Bay), and Peter Davi (Ghost Tree/Northern California) have passed away in extreme surfing conditions. Multi-wave hold-downs, severe coral reef injuries, and entangled leashes are common causes of death in Big Wave surfing. Says Grant "Twiggy" Baker, "No matter how good you get, no matter how many hours you put in, you'll always pay these dues."[14]

Kenny "Skindog" Collins of Santa Cruz, CA, had to test his commitment and priorities in March 2011 when his good friend Sion Milosky died during a shared free-surf session at Maverick's. Collins saw Milosky's body on the beach that afternoon, and it took him several months before he felt prepared to go back into big surf again. "I've got a beautiful family to take care of. You don't get back in the game unless you truly love it," said Collins.[15]

That's sage advice for the would-be entrepreneur. Too many entrepreneurs get blinded by their "vision" or dream or worse still by their sense of entitlement and lose touch with reality. Too often they are unable to be strategic about what to do and when to do it.. Too often they are unable to be strategic in what to do and when to do it. The ability to prioritize and the desire to get frequent and honest criticism and feedback will help you know when you are ready to get back in the game.

Most Big Wave surfers pay their dues daily and head right back out ASAP. Bumps, bruises, a few torn ligaments and stitches here and there, maybe some super-glue on a cut or duct tape on a dinged board . . . then right back out they go.

"I remember coming over the top of one wave and then, as happens regularly out there, another is getting ready to break about 50 feet outside of us," says Greg Long. "It was probably about 25 feet on the face and this thing landed right on top of me. At first, when I saw it, there was that moment of panic but then I thought, 'You can do this, don't worry,'" he says. "Going through the whole rag-dolling motion, getting dragged under water, coming up and taking a couple more, getting washed by the rocks to the inside and coming out the other side and being okay." Then he adds, "It's kind of weird, but I think you'll get most Big Wave surfers to admit it that there are times that

75

walking away from a horrendous wipeout can almost feel better than having made a wave. It forces you into a whole other frame of mind. Instinctively you want to panic and freak out but you know that you can't."[16]

Steve Jobs's life story is well known. He faced failure often and managed to land on his feet more often than not. Before he dropped out of Reed College, out of curiosity he decided to take a calligraphy class. He learned about typefaces and spacing between letters, information which did not at the time seem to have any practical value. But a decade later when he was designing the first Macintosh computer, he remembered things he learned in that class and created the first computer with multiple typefaces and spacious fonts. So there is always more to be learned that may serve you well later.

PREPARE FOR FEAR

For the vast majority of Big Wave surfers the risks are known . . . and faced. Wave choice is crucial in huge surf in part because it is the classic intersection of fear countered by preparation. As old-school surfing legend Buzzy Trent said, "Waves aren't measured in feet, but in increments of fear."[17] And by analogy, the bigger the challenge, the greater the preparation. You can prepare to face your fears just as you prepare for anything else.

Reflecting on one of the biggest waves he ever took, champion Big Wave surfer Grant "Twiggy" Baker said, "It was such a fine line between being stuck in that lip and somehow making it. The parallel universes that splintered off from there gave my life a whole different direction. There was no planning . . . it was just pure f#*%ing terror. No flotation back then, bad leashes, crazy. I can't really even remember the day, or that wave, really. Fear was just the overwhelming sense.

"But I do remember a moment of that wave—again, another split second. As I started paddling for it, there was a little ramp at the top that forced my board onto the inside edge and it started to track to the right, which basically was going to take me over the falls, in the lip, while I was still lying on my board. I was saying, 'Oh my God, oh my God,' and then finally it corrected itself. That was a moment where things could have gone completely wrong."

But wait, there's more. "I also remember the moment after my bottom turn. I was looking for the barrel, because that's what we were doing all day, looking for the barrel on that second section, but I could see it was kind of crumbling and I wasn't going to make it, so I straightened in front of it," he recalls. "I remember the foam coming over me and thinking, 'Okay, you're done, never going to survive this foamy,' but the foam shot over me and didn't touch me inside, no pressure on me whatsoever, and I was like 20 feet deep inside it, no pressure at all, then boom, out the front, on a 55-footer."[18]

Every entrepreneur has those pivotal moments facing barriers as well. For some, the moment comes early when they first broach an idea to a friend or colleague who immediately fire-hoses it with statements like, "That'll never work," or "That's been tried before," or "Who will fund *that*?" For others, turning points come when the process is underway and a main client is late paying an invoice and there is no cash flow readily at hand. Or, the moment comes when they have to decide whether to keep working from a home office or to move into a larger, more formal space. Each of these moments can be fearful at the least and terrifying at the worst. How you deal with these situations often determines the eventual success of your endeavor.

For Big Wave surfers, the scale is magnified and the stakes very high. Pedro Calado at Puerto Escondido, Mexico, had a pivotal moment on May 3, 2015: "I felt like I was in a nightmare.

When I hit the water the first time, I felt my life vest rip. I skipped and tumbled and hit two more times before the wave finally swallowed me. At this point, my life vest was actually almost entirely off of me. I held on to it with all of my strength," he says. "Eventually I hit the sand at the bottom, and was able to gather which way was up and to get to the surface. I don't remember how long it was, . . . just that it was way too long . . . I almost died and broke a brand-new board; it was rough." Later, though, came a modicum of redemption. "Once I started seeing photos and hearing from others that my wave was one of the biggest ever paddled into at Puerto, I actually got really happy! After all, I don't think it was *that* bad [laughs]. And yes, I will be back out there soon."[19]

IT'S NOT ABOUT TALENT

"I was terrified of Big Waves when I was small," says Australian surfer Mark Matthews. "My mum would have to come and rescue me on a bodyboard when I was stuck out the back. Pretty embarrassing, really. It's not about talent. I was never especially talented when I was young. There were loads of kids at Maroubra that would beat me in the local competitions, so I was never that good. I mean I'm not that good now, to be honest. I've just made a career from taking off on waves that other people don't want to take off on." Not a bad entrepreneurial strategy either.

In 2001, he surfed Shipsterns Bluff in Tasmania, "which was relatively unknown and by far the biggest waves I had ever surfed. The biggest thing that came from that experience was that I was hooked. I went from being really scared of Big Waves to taking the biggest leap you could take in surfing at the time. After that, I couldn't even find waves that were big enough to scare me . . . It was just a massive jump-start."

His jump-start carried over into business for him, as well. "In some ways, maybe I'm a lot better at the business side of surfing than I am at the surfing side of surfing. I've learned that there are parallels to being a Big-Wave surfer and being successful at the business and marketing side. It's like I've done a marketing business degree over the last decade. You actually know more than you think."

He adds, "It all comes down to hard work. I was never supertalented, so I figured out every way I could do to get paid more than I deserve. And that comes down to just hard work. That's about it, really. Do the hard work and hopefully the rewards will come."[20]

When you push the edge, the hard work of recovering from a fall is physical, mental, and emotional. I asked professional Big Wave surfer Nic Lamb about patience and fear; whether the former is factored into his preparation and the latter is disregarded to a greater extent than most would. Nic responded, "Patience is something I'm constantly trying to reach for. I don't know if someone in my position ever reaches optimal patience, but I think the process is you do get restless and cranky and tiresome and eager. Patience, that's what I'm going for. It may not seem that way, but I am very patient. Very, very patient. Very, very patient. I feel in the next year or so I'll be able to collect a few of the things that I've been looking to get." Prophetically, six months after he told me this he won the Titans of Mavericks contest.

As for fear, Nic told me, "Chasing larger swells, we are able to spot the feeling [of fear] and kinda capture it and use it to our advantage, as opposed to someone who it kinda creeps up on them . . . and they don't know how to use it and they have the nervous energy. Whereas when I have the nervous energy I know it's time to 'go.' Everything I've been preparing for, waiting for, for weeks, months, years I use that energy and it keeps me sharper. Makes me better. Things slow down. I'm able to control the situation more. So I welcome that feeling."[21]

For the successful entrepreneur and innovator, there are times when "things slow down" as well, in the face of large challenges and opportunities. Most of the great entrepreneurs I have known have some way of reducing stress. For some it is yoga, or a long walk, or playing a musical instrument for a few minutes. These are ways to take a beep breath and regroup. Similarly, when facing a new and perhaps dazzling opportunity, managing expectations is more important that managing stress. In this case, to slow things down might entail double-checking the numbers or running a pilot project in order to regain some control of your emotions.

THE OCEAN NEVER TAKES THE DAY OFF

In the last 20 years, more and more women have entered the water to face big waves with the same proportion of rides and wipeouts as the men. "I think anyone who says they aren't scared in big waves is just crazy!" says Paige Alms. "It's about overcoming that fear and turning it into adrenaline."[22] Sometimes, it boils down to the Japanese proverb: *Fall seven times, stand up eight.*

"I've been surfing . . . since I was about 12, so I've put in a lot of time," says Keala Kennelly. "Being a Big Wave surfer . . . I've taken my fair share of beatings, so for sure it helps to not be intimidated when the conditions are heavy."[23]

As mentioned earlier, Brazil's Maya Gabeira is one of the best-known female Big Wave surfers in the world. For example, she won the ESPY award in 2009 as the Best Female Action Sports Athlete, and the following year she was named top Female Action Sports Athlete at the Teen Choice Awards. As

Greg Long says, "Gabeira's Big-Wave credentials are practically unimpeachable." She has spent thousands of hours in the water. She's devoted months to towing and paddling into nearly all the world's biggest breaks. She has strengthened her lungs, and she can hold her breath for nearly five minutes if she stays relaxed. "She has dedicated her life to managing these risks," says Long.[24]

So how does she manage risks? It all starts with preparation. Sponsored for some time by Red Bull, she recently sent them a long, detailed safety-equipment wish list that included wetsuits with flotation, custom-fitted helmets for impact resistance, GPS, and color-track pigment; a rescue loop; life vests with CO_2 cartridges; oxygen tanks for their Jet Ski plus training on how to use them; a second 1,800-horsepower jet ski equipped with oxygen bottles; knee and elbow pads for surfing shallow reef breaks; and an advanced radio, so that the jet-ski drivers could be in constant contact with each other and the emergency team on the shore.

Garrett McNamara, who by some accounts, via tow-in, has ridden the largest wave ever recorded (about 100 feet), has his long list as well. "Talk with all the locals," he begins. "Minimum, you have to have a safety driver and somebody on the cliff with binoculars and walkie-talkie. That's just to go in the water. When we go out we also have a fire truck, an ambulance, a lifeguard, and then our own quad with our own safety guy runnin' around." He adds, "And . . . we have five people on the cliff with walkie-talkies, spotting . . . You can definitely catch the biggest wave of your life out there . . . It's not really even surfing, it's more survival."[25]

As Long says, "Eventually, every surfer falls. When you fall, it's not up to you when you come up." Nature always wins. The ocean never takes the day off. The wave will hold you down and roll you around as long as it pleases.

Maya Gabeira learned this the hard way during her now-legendary wipeout in Nazaré, Portugal.

81

Reflecting on that day she says, "I wouldn't do it again. I took a very, very big chance, especially with losing the radio and going anyway. But I don't regret it, not even a little bit. It was the most enriching experience of my life. I learned and changed so much in that nine minutes. I think the only reason I was able to do that is because I had trained so hard and dedicated so much time and passion toward that one goal," she says. "That's why I survived. Now I know better, and I'm a different person. And I like this person better."[26]

For the entrepreneur, as for Maya, it is vitally important to learn from your mistakes. Perhaps you got bad advice from a supposedly good consultant. Time to make a change. Perhaps your revenue projections were too optimistic. Make a revised budget. Or maybe you have realized you have the right person in the wrong role. Make a move and align the person and role. In all these examples, closing the doors is not an option.

YOU HAVE A CHOICE

Shaun Tomson has taken his share of falls and major league wipeouts, many in an era of surfing that had little technology and even less safety equipment. I asked him about falling:

"Metaphorically, how do you look at wipeouts? And what lessons from them do you apply to business?"

"Well, you can look at that as a learning experience. You can look at it as something that is an inevitable result of pushing yourself to the absolute limit," he said. "If you don't fall sometimes, you haven't pushed yourself to your limit. It's only when you wipe out that you come to that realization that I'm gonna push myself even more.

"I have a choice. I can paddle in or I can paddle back out. And are you someone who paddles in or paddles back out?

Perseverance is sort of at the core of entrepreneurial business. It's sort of a cycle: fall, paddle back out, ride. You sort of keep going through that wonderful, rhythmical thing."[27]

There are only a few Big Wave surfers who rarely fear *fear*. They do, however, face choices. And if they had a choice between a Big Wave off-shore and a Big Wave close in, they'd take off-shore. San Francisco's Mark "Doc" Renneker explains why.

"Fear was never an issue. I somehow am missing that fear gene. Well, that isn't 100 percent accurate. Being a doctor and doing surf medicine stuff, I see people who have broken their necks surfing, and it's always in shallow, shore break. I actually am afraid of shallow, hard breaking waves," he says. "If I get pulled over the falls on some little shallow, shore break wave, I get scared."

With the stoic logic of a physician, that's not all that scares him. "I'm scared of other surfers' Big Wave boards. Because that's a great way to get a significant head injury," he says. "If fear is something that you hold in your mind in anticipation of something bad happening, I don't hold that in my mind. I don't see that kind of peril in surf, no matter how big it gets. But that's a function of learning over many years how to safely be in big surf."

So Doc Renneker's preparation is a little different than many of his peers. He expects occasional wipeouts, so he of course studies the conditions. Then he visualizes, plans exit strategies, and trains accordingly. "To acquire that sort of experience or knowledge, to understand the place, took a lot of time. Really surfing the biggest days here (at Maverick's), when the outer bars area is breaking, edging out, edging out, edging out, learning what these offshore currents do, and the tides, the swell direction, wind. And then rehearsing, as it were, even over the summertime, just having the fun of speed paddling out a mile and just swimming back with your board behind you. Rehearsing all the escape routes."

Always strategic, he made many mental emergency plans of " . . . getting caught in a rip, all the things that can happen in surfing—two-wave hold-downs and whatever else—and I would seek out those experiences." Yes, you read that correctly, he would *seek out* those experiences. "I used to rehearse two-wave hold-downs. I used to stay down for two waves on purpose, just to ablate the fear, because what I know of fear is that it will increase your heart rate, and it will increase your oxygen usage, and you won't last as long."

For the entrepreneur, the power of visualization and of building scenarios cannot be overestimated. Many of the best entrepreneurs I know are great list makers. As they think of something, they jot it down. Even if there is no particular or immediate use, they keep it for future reference. They build various scenarios, too, as they become more and more familiar with an industry, a market, the competition and their own product or service.

Doc's introduction to Maverick's came via Jeff Clark. "When I first went out there in 1990, to Jeff's credit, he was fully formed in his knowledge of Maverick's. I mean, he really knew the place. For however many times he surfed it, he'd learned the place."

To prepare for Maverick's Doc had to recalibrate not only his mind, but also his own metabolism. ". . . So when I drive, every time—this may sound obsessive or OCD or something—but virtually every time I drive to Maverick's, from the beginning, from 1991 on, I would do this thing at the start of the air strip heading south. I'll drive only 35 miles per-hour, not past the speed limit, and I'll hold my breath for the length of that road." At that speed he is holding his breath about two minutes. "So . . . when I really want to breathe, I'll let off on the accelerator, down to 30, 20, and it seems to take forever, and that's what simulates a long hold-down. Much as you want to get to the surface, you just have to wait. You can definitely, as it were, uncouple or desensitize a superficial fear response."[28]

This kind of rehearsal is part of the preparation. I have created and taught seminars for innovators and entrepreneurs for over 25 years. For example, in my *Innovating for Results*™ seminar, I make it a point to have them put together a 30-second description of their idea, product, or service that is clear and easy to understand. Then I have them memorize it, rehearse it, and deliver it to others in attendance so they will be ready when the time comes to speak their piece in earnest.

Clearly, one size of preparation and training does not fit all. I have heard that Bianca Valenti, who lives in Marin County just north of San Francisco, gets ready for Big Waves by holding her breath the full length of the Golden Gate Bridge (about three to four minutes) as part of her training routine. Most Big Wave surfers find their own personal recipes for dealing with fear. Preparation is certainly a constant. Studying local conditions is, too. And having state of the art equipment and a high-quality team is a given, as well. Some, though, are not nearly as cerebral about facing fear as Doc or Bianca.

At the Salvation Army Aquatics Center in San Diego, acclaimed Big Wave surfers like Damien Hobgood, Josh Kerr, Taylor Knox, and Jojo Roper took a Waterman Survival course that would make a Navy SEAL proud. For example, they swam multiple laps holding their breath until their lips were blue from CO_2 in the bloodstream. For safety, this is done in pairs because you can actually lose consciousness and not realize it.

They then did an exercise called "touch-and-go's," which required them to dive down, touch the bottom, return to the surface, and repeat over and over. At times a little "push and shove" from their buddies underwater was added to simulate the jostling you get under a huge wave after a wipeout.

Why train like this? "Everyone who surfs serious waves has experienced [serious wipeouts]," says instructor Mark Lozano. "You get pushed down to the bottom by a wave, you fight back to the surface, and all of a sudden the next wave is right on top of you. Our goal is to make this class as true to life as possible," he says. With some reality-based levity he adds that Big Wave surfer "Mike Stewart gave us some input and recommended we make them jump off the diving board onto the concrete, and then roll into the pool and hold their breath. He thought that would be the most realistic."

The preparation and training definitely helps physically and mentally. "As long as I maintain that confident feeling in Big Waves, I'm fine," says Lozano. "It's when I start overthinking that things go wrong . . . After all, maintaining a relaxed state allows you to conserve oxygen and roll with the watery punches."

Preparation and training often jumpstart confidence, which is crucial to Big Wave surfing success. "It feels good to get that confidence boost," says Lozano. "But it's just as important to actually change your physiology if you want to surf serious waves, and that takes focus and training over the long run." In the "survival notes" for the course is perhaps the most practical advice: "Before going under a big wave, remain calm and take as many successive deep breaths as possible before diving."[29]

Matt Bromley grew up near Cape Town, South Africa.

Graduating from small wave to Big Wave surfing came naturally to him. Maybe it was peer-pressure or maybe adrenaline, but either way he was on a mission. He paddled hard, dropped in and then, "I realized that I was way too deep as soon as I bottom turned and I knew that I was in trouble. My worst nightmare was realized."

His vivid description resembles hundreds of similar ones that every Big Wave surfer can offer up: "The foam ball grabbed me, threw me, and sent me deep . . . Then I hit the reef and tumbled all over it . . . I came up just as the next one landed on my head. Then another. Then another. I was getting seriously beaten as every wave unloaded on me." Prepare as he may, he would never know if he prepared enough until tested, a lesson for every entrepreneur and innovator to learn as well.

"Five waves later, chunks of coral heads started popping up outside of me and I knew that I was on top of the ledge. I had so much adrenaline going that I didn't even care. I ended up getting sucked all the way over the dry reef, through a gully and back into the channel. I somehow survived."

Having come out alive, he then had to paddle back to the boat. When he got there, "I got such a rush from it and the boys were all cheering. It felt so good." When you expect to recover, learn, and return to the fray, you are ready for the next one. "For me, that was the ultimate wave. Hopefully *next* time I can make it."[30]

Jack Viorel, founder of Wrightsville, North Carolina's Indo Jax Surf School and Indo Jax Surf Charities, introduces underprivileged kids to the joys and lessons of surfing. He says what surfing teaches is deeper—and wider—than any ocean. "Even the best surfers wipe out—a lot. Getting good at surfing means a ton of wipeouts. To many of the kids we work with, their lives seem like a wipeout," he says. "Surfing teaches that wipeouts are just part of the deal. When you learn to wipe out and go back out, that can translate to your own life. You can wipe out in anything you're doing, but all you have to do is paddle back out."[31]

To be an effective player in business means you have to keep pushing and learning. You also have to stay positive and assume you have what it takes to win. Many a startup fails because the founders unwittingly and/or unconsciously expected it to fail.

EARN THE WAVE

Originally, this chapter was going to be called "Expect to Wipe Out Daily." I had done a few interviews, and that title seemed reasonable because it spoke to rallying after falling, something every entrepreneur and start-up has to reckon with. But over time, more and more of the Big Wave surfers offered another point of view that helped me change mine.

Jeff Clark told me, "I don't *expect* to wipe out . . . *ever*! But do I push the edge to a point where that *could* happen? I hope so. Always," he said. "A wipeout will give you a better understanding of what you need to do differently to be successful. Being in condition and prepared well enough is essential for your survival. But a lot of times the wipeouts are a mental thing, not so much a physical thing. They can become physical . . . I've come up purple before. And my friends are like, 'How long have you been down?' and I'm like, 'I don't know . . . long enough to get purple.'

"It's knowing that you have that mindset that will let you hold out for a wipe out," he adds. "People ask me, 'How long can you hold your breath?' and it's always been 'As long as I have to.' That's how long I can hold my breath. And knock on wood, it hasn't failed me ever."[32]

No one gets the perfect ride on the perfect wave on the perfect day. So, it is important to be resilient and to learn from each wave as well as every wipeout. Surfers physically *prepare* to fall. For the entrepreneur, remaining agile and holding several options open serves a purpose. If you are agile, you and your company can change often and in targeted ways in our fast-forward world. There is nothing wrong with having a Plan B, or C, or M, either.

Nic Lamb told me, "It's not so much 'Expect to wipe out daily,' but to prepare for one. And in preparation and constantly working hard towards your goals, making sure physically you're as fit as you can be, and mentally you're as sharp as you can be, you'll be able to reach your maximum potential. It starts with the swimming, then you get stronger, you start eating healthier . . . and in turn, as you get healthier physically it helps you mentally," he says. "You know you're doing everything that you can. I also work with high-stakes sports psychologist Nick Curson at Speed of Sports, . . . so, yeah, there's some mental training you can do, as well. Visualization is key, but a good starting point is make sure you're sound physically."[33]

I spoke to Nick Curson to get his perspective on elite athletes in general. He told me that they are "old souls with a strong sense of identity at an early age." Himself a surfer, he plans an intense workout regimen for Nic based on the length of competitive heats of 45 minutes. When I asked him about what similarities he sees between successful athletes and successful business people when it comes to dealing with setbacks, he said, "the biggest factors are sacrifice, perseverance and mental toughness. "

Learning from your mistakes is an old adage that every business school professor or sports coach hammers into their students. Still, mistakes are often thought of as errors to be avoided, even feared. To entrepreneurs, as to surfers, mistakes are viewed very differently: as a fertile ground for learning faster than the competition. Taking smart risks is imperative. To be smart, though, requires discipline: to check and double check, to listen continuously to your customers and emerging market trends, and to adjust accordingly.

For innovators, failures are just a precursor to the next iteration. Fail often; learn often. Innovators needn't think in terms of successes and failures—that's a false dichotomy. To innovators, *iterations* matter. And what is iteration? It is essentially movement forward via failures and revisions. Innovators, like surfers expect to make mistakes—and . . . even will make them *intentionally*—. . . so as to gain a new perspective or insight or solution to a problem.

As we will see in the next chapter, complacency in the face of success is a recipe for disaster. As the surfers say, "Never turn your back on the ocean."

PADDLE BACK OUT

No one gets the perfect ride on every wave. So, it is important to be resilient and to learn from each wave. Surfers prepare in various ways for wipeouts and falls, so that they can
paddle back out and try again. A "wipe out" is a great learning opportunity. To paddle back out to face the next wave is
almost, at times, triumphant.

Big Wave surfing warrior Ken Bradshaw tells it like it is:
"To get beat up by a wave, survive it, and get up to do it
again in the space of 15 minutes is as much about physical
conditioning as it is about mental toughness. There's no way
a lay person could ever understand what it feels like, but if I
were to describe it I would say that it feels like getting hit by
a car, a soft car, and then spun around in a washing ma-
chine," he says. "This all happens in complete darkness, so
that once you stop spinning you're presented with the challenge of finding your equilibrium and figuring out which way
is up. Not to mention the pressure change: You can be
pushed from the water's surface 50 feet down in less than a
second, which is a pressure change of two atmospheres." As
if that weren't enough he adds "If you survive the pounding
of one wave, you can be hit by a second one in less than 20
seconds, and then a third can pull you down into what we
call a 'triple hold.' Getting held underneath the water by three
waves is probably the maximum that a person can take and
still survive. I've only known two people who successfully
negotiated a triple hold. After that, you're out of luck."[34]

Surfer Richard Woolcott suffered a broken neck at the age
of 19 after a wave slammed him into a sandbar. With his

dream of being a professional surfer shattered, Woolcott was forced to redirect his career plans. Once a sponsored surfer for Quiksilver, Woolcott knew he had to change directions; his familiarity with retail clothing lines led to him leaving professional surfing to form his own brand, Volcom, in 1991. Woolcott and his friend Tucker Hall started Volcom as a clothing company that would embody everything they loved about surfing, skating, and snowboarding. Never complacent, they went on to expand into making numerous action DVDs via Volcom Entertainment, then on to their own record label, and most recently to helping fans and athletes showcase artwork on websites. All of these ventures draw upon lessons learned from surfing and helped Woolcott build Volcom into the success it is today.

To push the edge will inevitably mean you will tumble off that ledge on occasion. And the pattern will repeat itself over and over: push the limits, fall, learn, and paddle back out. Consider the wisdom of billionaire inventor Sir James Dyson: "Being an entrepreneur, an inventor, is about having ideas and the doggedness to see them through." Unable to get funding for his brainchild of a better vacuum cleaner, he developed and manufactured his vacuum under his own name. "Innovators shouldn't be afraid to take risks. They should embrace failure and learn from their mistakes. I created 5,127 prototypes of the first bagless vacuum cleaner, and only the last one was right!"[35]

Even when you think you have learned and applied all you can, when you decide to not mess with success, your complacency is setting you up for failure. As Steve jobs said, "Stay hungry. Stay foolish."[36]

THINGS TO DO:

In business, as in surfing, there will always be victories and setbacks. For the entrepreneur this process is often magnified and happens more frequently because decisions have to be made quickly and with fewer resources. This can take a toll on confidence, so it is helpful to recall instances when you have been knocked down and gotten back up.

In my consulting work, I encourage entrepreneurs to keep a "Plan B Log." It is a simple process:

1. Look back over time and write down any number of times when you tried something that didn't work, your Plan A.

2. Next to each entry, write what you learned from this and what you did that was successful— your Plan B.

3. Keep a running list in your Log, and when times get tough, take it out and read it to yourself. Your resilience will provide you with encouragement as you face the next Plan A setback, learn from it, and paddle back out via Plan B.

7
NEVER TURN YOUR BACK ON THE OCEAN

SO MUCH OF WHAT WE KNOW ABOUT CATCHING AND RIDING big waves has its origins in the Hawaiian and Polynesian cultures. From the "reading" of a wave, to the position in the lineup, to the mental and spiritual preparation, all have their roots in the South Pacific where the people know and respect the ocean. This knowledge and respect has been passed down from generation to generation. So, from their earliest moments at the beach, Hawaiian parents can be heard telling their children "Mai Huli`oe I Kokua o Ke Kai"—never turn your back on the ocean.

This cautionary phrase contains within it multiple nuances and messages. The ocean is so powerful, so unpredictable even, that being on constant alert is mandatory. Just when you think you are safe in waist-high water, a riptide can give you a free ride out to sea. Its power and energy is so potent it can knock your legs out from under you and take your breath away. Or maybe you are simply fishing on a rock by the sea, with your ice chest, bait bucket, and beach chair minding your own business when *wham*, a rogue wave comes through and next thing you know you are eating more sand than fish.

I remember on my first trip to Oahu's Waikiki Beach coming upon a large bronze statue of Duke Kahanamoku. Bigger than life, with arms outstretched, leis around his neck and arm, and a longboard towering over him, the tribute statue was bold and beautiful. But, it had one flaw: Duke's back was to the ocean. I had wondered about that until I read Stuart Holmes Coleman's book *Eddie Would Go*: " . . . Some watermen believe the statue is facing in the wrong direction. City officials and the Kahanamoku family approved placing it facing the street so tourists could take pictures of the Duke with the blue ocean in the background," says Coleman. "But as . . . most lifeguards know, you should never turn your back to the sea. This is not only out of respect for the god of the ocean, who can be fickle and dangerous, but it is also a practical precaution. Like any experienced waterman, Duke knew what could happen when you took your eye off the sea or underestimated its power."[1]

In my strategic consulting work with businesses over the past 30 years, I often begin projects by telling clients to "Never turn your back on the customer." It always surprises me how often people who should know better take their eye off that which can sustain them, teach them, and nurture them: their customers. I learned this lesson from surfing, and have applied it to business ever since. Entrepreneurs often forget that their customers are not a static entity or some demographic category. Customers, end-users, clients, and guests change all the time. Long-gone are the days when one size fits all—now one size fits one. So constant vigilance is a competitive advantage.

In the tradition of Duke, legendary lifeguard and Big Wave surfer Eddie Aikau knew better than most about vigilance and the ocean's power. Working as a lifeguard, he was a local legend for how many times he charged into dangerous seas and for how many lives he saved. He came to the aid of sunburned tourists and skilled surfers in massive North Shore surf. His fearless rescues are still the basis of long "talk story" conversations. Never one to mince words, Eddie told it like it is: "I will never understand the stupidity of people who turn their backs on the ocean. People who have no knowledge of the danger the ocean threatens will walk right into it backwards while snapping pictures of the family. One wave and—ZAP—they are grabbed and sucked out in seconds."[2]

To Eddie and many others, the ocean has a personality of its own. It has its moods, its quirks, its ever-changing tastes and ways. The best innovators and inventors understand this about customers and clients, as well. Customers can be fickle and hard to predict. The ocean, like customers, has a mind of its own that is worth paying attention to. You can't afford to take it for granted.

IF IN DOUBT, DON'T GO OUT

Every town or village near the ocean faces challenges when it comes to protecting people from their own stupidity. Every search and rescue volunteer, every EMT, and every lifeguard working near the sea tries to warn and educate the public about local conditions by posting notices and offering warnings galore. For example, on one Maui beach there is specific instruction saying: "Respect the Ocean: Always respect the power of the ocean. Do not go out in conditions beyond your abilities. No matter how good you are, there will always be conditions beyond your abilities. Never turn your back on the ocean. Keep an eye on the incoming waves. Beware of rogue waves and freak waves. There are commonly extra-large waves in a set or just occasionally, we call these 'clean up sets' or rogue waves. Check the ocean conditions with the lifeguards and surf forecasters. Seek advice from more experienced surfers."

The last words offer the best and most succinct advice: "If in doubt, don't go out!"[3]

Far too many who come to the beach and head into the ocean have a limited purview of the many things about the ocean to watch out for. They forget that the ocean is about much more than what you see on the surface of the water. It's important to have an understanding of what is under, on, and above the ocean as well: from rip currents to coral reefs to sharks to jelly fish, not to mention the quality of the water itself.

There is a three dimensionality to the axiom "Never turn your back on the ocean." The power of the ocean is not restricted to what you see with your eyes. There is so much to know about what is under, on, and above the sea. Again, the analogy to business rings true. If the customer is like the ocean, knowing the customers values, tastes, and trends will determine the success— or failure—of your endeavor. If you lose in-depth touch with the customer, you can very quickly get into deep trouble.

GET BACK OUT THERE

Now comes the hardest question for Big Wave surfers, as well as for entrepreneurs and startups: If—no, *when*—you have a massive wipeout or suffer a major setback, do you give up or do you, as a surfer buddy of mine puts it, "get your ass back out there?" Do you turn your back on the ocean, . . . never to return? Or do you turn yourself around and head back into the action?

Four of the most heavily discussed incidents in recent surfing history involved a rampaging wave, a coral reef, and two great white sharks. In each case, the surfers had near-death experiences, and in each case in time they found a way to paddle back out again. Let's look at these in more detail: Maya Gabeira's massive wipeout at Nazarè, Portugal; Keala Kennelly's face pounding on the coral reef at Teahupo'o; Mick Fanning's encounter with a great white shark at Jeffreys Bay in South Africa; and Bethany Hamilton's loss of her arm to a shark near Tunnels Beach in Ha'ena, Kauai.

Maya at Nazaré:
Enduring Brave and Horrible Moments

As mentioned earlier, Maya Gabeira attempted to ride a behemoth wave at Nazaré, Portugal, in 2013. With her long time mentor Carlos Burlé driving the Jet Ski, Maya was towed in to one of the biggest waves of any day or any year for any gender. She caught the wave and headed down its face, hitting three massive bumps hard. She then selected her angle when *bam*, the wave caught her and a monumental thrashing began. Held down for two to three minutes, she came up gasping for air, and then was hit twice more by the ensuing waves. At great personal risk, Carlos went into the 30-foot high white water and was able to get to her and get her ashore where she collapsed on the sand. Dramatic footage showed Carlos and others giving her CPR on the beach. She was then taken to the hospital where, among other things, she found out that the bumps she hit on the face of the wave were the likely cause of a broken ankle. She later said that she was not aware of the ankle injury because of the excruciating pain from her lungs and chest after the long hold-downs.

About a year and a half later, I was able to talk to Maya at length about the events of that day.

"A lot of people don't understand how anybody in their right mind would go into Big Waves like you do with your mentor Carlos," I said. "They think it's just crazy, or just adrenaline or thrill-seeking. What do you tell people about why you two keep chasing those waves?"

"Yeah, it's [about us] searching for Big Waves, him putting a lot of time into me, developing me as a Big Wave surfer," she said. "And I think for us, nine years later, to see ourselves in waves that big and challenging, and for me, to obviously be the first one on the rope, and get a wave that big, survive what I survived, and have him save me and then see him go back out and catch the wave [later that day] . . . I think it is pretty much the summary of our nine years, you know, [how we] battle together. A crazy experience and a lot, a *lot* of hard work, and difficulties, and brave and horrible moments. And I think it was just one of those days when everything that we do just got very exposed. And we lived at the very fullest and we lived that for nine years. And it just kind of hit a peak there.

"I think that is the reason why, in places like in Nazeré and in days like that, we really kind of shine and I feel more comfortable. It's just one of those days that God gives you the opportunity to just be yourself, and do your thing and not be under such pressure and so intimidated by others and the ocean."[4]

Seven months later, after her ankle healed, Maya returned to Big Wave surfing at Nazaré with no hesitation—and more importantly, with no regrets. Subsequently, she has been nominated for the Billabong and Tag Huer XXL Wave of the Year awards.

It is important for an entrepreneur to be persistent. For Maya, it was a nine-year journey. For a startup, it may be nine months. Knowing when the time is right is critical. And it is a valuable asset to have a trusted mentor. Too often I have seen young startups fail because they made the simplest of mistakes they were unaware of, mistakes that could have been avoided with even a modicum of good advice early on. A mentor knows you well enough to know your strengths and your weaknesses. And you know your chosen mentor well enough to trust him or her. A frank and honest relationship with frank and honest feedback will expedite entrepreneurial wins.

Keala at Teahupo'o:
Standing Up to Your Fears

Born and raised on the tranquil north side of Kauai, the "Garden Island" of the Hawaiian chain, Keala Kennelly is anything but tranquil. Tough as nails, she is a legend in the Big Wave and surfing community. She ranked in the Top 10 for more than a decade, won an X-Games gold medal, and was the first women to tow-in at Teahupo'o.

During a TedX Malibu talk she addressed what drives her to ride Big Waves. "When you ride inside a wave, you have the energy of all of that water swirling around you. You can feel the raw power of nature and it's one of the most exhilarating feelings you can take in . . . With a bigger wave the intensity of that feeling is multiplied," she says. "Time slows down. Some of your senses like smell, taste, and sound fade away. While others are so incredibly heightened, you feel like you have super human powers. Your sight has *pinpoint* precision focus. And your sense of touch is so amplified you can feel every drop of water on that wave . . . And when I get spit out of that wave I feel like I am the master of the universe." Then she quickly adds, "But

I'm not the master of the universe. So when that moment passes I go back to being a woman in a male-dominated sport."[5]

"The stuff guys are doing these days is seriously nuts," tweeted World Champion Kelly Slater. ". . . (going) into the oblivion not knowing what happens when you wipe-out. But the craziest guy of all is a girl . . . Looks like someone challenged her to a #YouWontGo contest and she called their bluff!"[6]

What Slater was referring to was a mountainous wave Keala took at Teahupo'o in 2015. This wave was not only the biggest of the day on one of the biggest days in memory, but it also signaled her return to the place where in 2011 she was seriously injured. As one commentator put it, "Kennelly knows full well the dangers of Teahupo'o, having been slammed face first into the reef by a wave."[7]

Photos of the right side of her face went viral when it happened. Had a Mack truck hit her, she would have looked better. The coral reef took a gruesome toll on her physically and mentally. "The injuries, which took dozens of stitches to repair, left Kennelly with posttraumatic stress disorder. She even started parting her hair on the opposite side because the touch of her fringe on the area of her face that was sliced open would make her jump."[8] Says Kennelly, "It felt like someone poured gasoline on my face and lit me on fire, it was such an intense pain."

It was two full years before the emotional and personal scars healed. "(Teahupo'o) is so intense—and so gorgeous—you can get the ride of your life out there, if you get the right one," she says. "To have an injury like that and to come back to that place was a huge personal triumph for me . . . I was beyond stoked. When stuff like that happens and you're able to overcome that and you're able to go back out there and stand up to your fears and succeed—there's something so empowering about that."[9]

Since the ocean never takes a day off, and in spite of the

personal victory it represented for Kennelly to go back out and face those Teahupo'o waves again, she managed to again get her fair share of abuse from the thick slabs of water upon her return. "I got the shit kicked out of me," she says. "My helmet blew off my head, I got whipped back over onto the reef onto the whole left side of my body and I thought I broke my hand. But all in all, I just have a couple scrapes and bruises. Considering the beating I got, I'm pretty unscathed."[10]

The marketplace never takes a day off and can be as brutal as a shallow coral reef. There have been two major global recessions in the last 15 years, and some have never recovered from these massive setbacks. But if you follow the Surfer's Rules to "Paddle Back Out," that itself is a small victory. Often what separates the victors from the vanquished in the marketplace is the ability to face a massive setback and give it another go. Agility and resilience enable the entrepreneur to carefully examine mistakes, correct them, develop a new plan, and move forward to implement it.

Mick at Jeffreys Bay: "Never Give Up, Never Give In"

On July 19, 2015, as millions of viewers watched live coverage of the World Surf League championship finals heat at Jeffreys Bay in South Africa, Australian surfer Mick Fanning experienced a terrifying shark attack. Fellow surfers gasped. Viewers were stunned. Even the seasoned commentator for the live video feed cried out "Holy shit!" as he realized what was happening. Within the hour, an estimated 30 million people had seen the footage showing a huge shark fin approaching him from behind on his left, circling him, then grabbing his leash and dragging him off his board—and he can be seen punching the shark as he slid off. Amazingly for Fanning's sake, the shark bit through the leash, thereby setting him free. The live coverage showed his competitor, Julian Wilson, heroically paddling *towards* him to help, as the rescue Jet Skis and safety boats raced in to gather him up.[11] Fanning escaped physical injury, but was emotionally ravaged. Relieved to be alive on shore, he broke down as he saw his fellow surfers approaching him with tears in their eyes. At that point the enormity of what had happened hit him. To the credit of the World Surf League organizers of the event, the final heat was cancelled, Fanning and Wilson were named co-champions, and the points and prize money was split between them.

Within a few days, a film crew from *60 Minutes Australia* accompanied Fanning as he returned to surf for the first time since the attack. As the *60 Minutes* segment aired, the opening words of the commentator mimicked those of many in the general public: "Mick Fanning is doing what many might think is completely mad: He's gone straight back into the water."[12]

"It's been almost a week now so it's like, it's time to get movin' again," said Fanning. "The longer you leave something the worse it'll get." His mom Liz told the commentator that in their family, "The motto is 'Never give up and never give in.' And he hasn't."[13]

The ocean, which has been his escape and his safe place since he started to surf at age four, now carries with it some additional fear. "When something like this happens, you're in your own mind. And your mind can play tricks on you. Your mind can turn shadows into demons. It's one of those things where you just gotta get back on the horse," said Fanning. "Things happen all the time and it's the way you react to them that sorta defines what they actually mean."[14]

The metaphorical sharks are lurking around every business endeavor, as well. These sharks take many forms: your direct competitors who challenge you for market share (e.g., Google vs. Netscape); the small, less expensive upstart (e.g., Quicken Loans); and the disruptive new product or technology that blindsides you and renders your product or service less viable (e.g., Uber and Airbnb).

Bethany at Tunnels Beach: Getting Back on the Board on Her Own Terms

Bethany Hamilton was 13 when her life changed one morning in late 2003. Born and raised on Kauai, she paddled out to Ha'ena's Tunnels Beach with her pro surfer friend Alana Blanchard, Alana's dad, and some other friends as she had done many times since she was four. Around 7:30 a.m., with numerous large sea turtles in the area, she was prone on her surfboard with her left arm in the water when a tiger shark attacked her, completely severing her left arm just below the shoulder. "It happened so fast there was no time to think. The shark had just taken my arm. I looked down and saw that my whole arm was gone."[15]

The Blanchards helped get her back to the beach where Alana's father made a tourniquet out of a surfboard leash and wrapped it around what remained of her arm. An ambulance was called and she was rushed to the closest hospital 45 minutes away. Bethany was known around the island to be a devout Christian, and in the ambulance one of the paramedics whispered in her ear "God will never leave you or forsake you."

As fate would have it, a skilled surgeon temporarily living in a hotel near the hospital was called and raced to tend to her. In a strange bit of coincidence, her father was scheduled to have knee surgery at the same hospital that morning, and she took his place in the operating room.

She spent a week in recovery before being released. During subsequent media interviews, she confirmed that she felt normal when she was bitten and did not feel much pain from the bite

103

at the moment of the disaster, but felt numb on the way to the hospital.

When the news broke of the shark attack, a family of local fishermen showed investigators photos of a 16-foot-long tiger shark they had caught and killed later that day about one mile from the attack site. It had surfboard debris in its mouth. When police compared measurements of its mouth with those of Hamilton's bitten board, it matched perfectly.

Now with one arm, Hamilton quickly decided to somehow return to surfing. Three weeks after the incident, her arm still bandaged, she was back in the water. She said she prayed before going back in "Dear Lord, keep me safe and everyone safe . . . and let my parents let me go out to where the real waves are . . . to just have fun!"[16]

She started with a custom-made board that was longer and slightly thicker than standard, with a handle for carrying with her right arm. She tried paddling in various ways, and learned to compensate by kicking more. "My first two waves I tried to get up . . . it was hard, and I was just trying to figure it out. My dad offered help and I was like, 'Nah, I'd rather do this on my own.'"[17] On the third wave, *boom* she got up!

Three months after the attack, after teaching herself anew to surf with one arm she entered a major competition on January 10, 2004. A year later she *won* the NSSA National Competition. In 2007, she *won* the Pipeline Women's Pro, and in 2014 she *won* the Surf n Sea Pipeline Women's Pro—all with one arm!

The broken and bitten surfboard that Hamilton was riding during the attack is on display at the California Surf Museum. The *soul surfer*, as she is called, decided that not only could she never walk away from the ocean, she also decided that she'd "rather do it my own way."

Every innovator faces moments when a vital part of a plan is under duress. It may be the sudden loss of funding, the unexpected departure of a key colleague, or the inability to access crucial materials and resources. This is why I always encourage clients to spend a fair amount of time looking at various "worst case" scenarios. By spending a little time anticipating problems, you gain momentum in solving those problems should they arise.

Maverick's pioneer Jeff Clark puts this all in perspective. "You have to be aware of everything. When we had the first (Maverick's) contest in 1999, I chose not to compete in the contest because I did not feel comfortable putting these guys out into a place that I know to be one of the most dangerous surf spots in the world, with a new water patrol, new people with (new) eyes on it. You have to look at this with seasoned eyes.

"My role had to be something I've always done, to see every moving part. Being able to see and count and have a mental record of everything that's moving. When I'm in the lineup, everything is data input. When I paddle into the lineup during a swell, every wave that comes through goes into a log, and averages, and so it's just the way I think about the ocean," he says. "And people go, 'How did you know the wave is gonna come through there?' And I say well, not every set, but every three sets there was one wave that was just kinda in a different place. When you assimilate a swell into your system like that you move involuntarily to those places because the conscious mind is not what's really driving it."[18]

So paying attention pays off. But over-thinking can be dangerous. Maverick's competitor Alex Martin says, "I definitely have the fear. My fear is (from) the respect I have for the ocean. In Maverick's, you know you can't think too much. You either go, or you don't . . . You don't want to be thinking because you might start thinking it's gonna be the last time I see my child."[19]

There are a wide range of options between meticulous preparation and intuitive free-styling. When it comes to riding Big

Waves, as with introducing a new product or service, you still have to have some chutzpah, some daring. You cannot rest on your laurels. Too often entrepreneurs are overly analytical, relying too much on left-brain logic, analysis, and data. Overthinking in these cases narrows your options, delays your entry point, and reduces your agility.

PROFIT MUST HAVE A PURPOSE

"Never mess with success" is one of the worst bits of advice you can give to a surfer or an entrepreneur. Constant adjustment is a requirement. Those who see the wave first and are the best prepared and positioned will enjoy the best ride. But the ocean is incessant and at times treacherous. There are undertows, currents, and riptides. And for the Big Wave surfers, there are longer and shorter intervals between waves that can be the deciding factor in whether to go for a certain wave or wait. In heavy surf conditions, if the interval between waves is too short the danger of a second or third wave breaking on you as you come up for air can be life-threatening.

The business bookshelves are filled with stories of companies that fell from the pedestals of commerce because they grew lazy, clumsy, and/or rigid. Woolworth's, Blockbuster, and Pan Am are just a few on a very long list of companies brought down by tunnel vision and complacency. They would have benefitted from understanding how the ocean operates. According to the Monterey Institute, "The sea is rarely still—row upon row of waves roll across its surface, seemingly endless and eternal."[20] So, too, in business: nothing is stationary, it is all in flux and moving. If you turn your back on the customer, the markets, or the new advances in technology, you are in danger.

Innovators are, in great measure, looking for opportunity where others have turned away. Innovators "Never Turn Their Back on the Ocean" and use this Surfer's Rule to their advantage. The challenge often for innovators is to pay attention to all aspects of the business and not lose sight of the supply chain, customer preferences, finances, etc. because they are singularly focused on product development. When "micro" issues are allowed to overshadow the "macro," in the process the "vision" can be lost.

I asked Shaun Tomson, "If you had one bit of advice to give to a young entrepreneur, what would it be?"

"I would say . . . you know, make a difference. Have a purpose. As an entrepreneur you understand, and you know, that there has to be profit. But profit without purpose . . . creating a difference . . . in the lives of your team, your community . . . that's where you get the sustainable juices. And business is moving in that direction, because big business is being held to a much higher standard by the consumer. They want to know the brands are supportive of the community, of the environment. It's not just about what's the profit gonna be in the next quarter," he said.

Then I offered, "Big corporations are trying to behave more entrepreneurially. Trying to mentally 'downsize.'"

"They want their team members and employees to listen to the power of one voice," Shaun said. "Many years ago when I was studying history, the history teacher, a wonderful man, was talking about social change. And he said it happens through the court . . . the court of public opinion! And today that court has a much, much bigger voice than it's ever had before. The court of public opinion rules the land."[21]

NEVER TURN YOUR BACK
ON THE OCEAN

No surfer is satisfied with one ride, and innovators or entrepreneurs should not be, either. To be sustainable is the name
of the game today. *Serial* entrepreneurs get serious attention
in the marketplace and from the investment community. For
savvy investors like Tugboat Ventures—working with those
who have a track record, and who take the long view is the
new normal.

The ocean is incessant and at times treacherous, and so
is the marketplace. Surfers contend with many factors beyond their control. Today, nothing is stationary; everything is
in flux and moving. If you turn your back on the customer, the
markets, the trends, or the new advances in technology, you
are in danger.

A narrow focus can be fatal. As surfer and businessman
Ben Martin says, "When you're starting a business, it's so
easy to let it become your world. Tunnel vision kicks in and
you can't think of anything except the next list of potential
clients you've got to email or what a blogger said about you
on Twitter. Here's where surfers have an advantage. A little
time spent in the ocean reminds you that there's a much
bigger world out there; that you're just a tiny part of it. That
kind of perspective can be helpful when you're stressing
about how many Facebook likes you got this week."[22]

Innovators use The Surfer's Rules to their advantage. Innovators are, in great measure, looking for opportunity where
others have turned their backs. Often the challenge for

innovators is to pay attention to all aspects of the business, not just the sexy new product under development.

THINGS TO DO:

Kevin Starr, in the *Stanford Social Innovation Review*, succinctly identified questions innovators and entrepreneurs must incessantly ask themselves regarding their product or service, in order to never turn their backs on customers. On a regular basis ask yourself:

1. Is it needed?

2. Does it work?

3. Will people use it as designed?

4. Will it get to those who need it most?

"The four questions are unforgiving; getting a no on any one of them means you won't pass go on your way to impact," says Starr. "That doesn't mean that a no answer should lead you to abandon the whole effort, but it should refocus your efforts on getting to yes."[23] Sometimes, getting to "yes" means you have to dare big!

8

DARE BIG

"IF YOU WANT TO PUSH YOUR PERFORMANCE LEVELS, FIND the relevant edge," write business gurus John Hagel and John Seely Brown. "In the case of Big Wave surfers, there has been an ever-expanding search for the breaks that would produce bigger and rougher waves to test new board designs and surfing practices."[1] Hagel and Brown are on to something, something special and instructive about the mindset of Big Wave surfers: If you're going to find that edge and push the limits, you might as well dare big!

If nothing else, Big Wave surfers by definition always dare big. Every wave is a major challenge, every set unique, and every swell a new danger . . . and a new opportunity. So it's no wonder that innovators and entrepreneurs have a lot to learn from them. "Surfing may seem a million miles from traditional business practice. But the evolution of the sport can provide invaluable insight into the innovation process."[2]

Hagel and Brown's insights into the links between surfing and business can help us move to the next level. It is no surprise that most of the Big Wave surfers are actively involved in the design, creation, and/or testing of new equipment as well as new strategies and techniques. From modified boards and fins to more powerful Jet Skis to inflatable safety vests, innovation is a given in the Big Wave surfing community.

The remainder of this chapter looks at how innovation, partnering with change, and taking smart risks are among the most fundamental tenets of The Surfer's Rules that guide entrepreneurs and innovators.

VESTED INTERESTS

As we have seen, Jeff Clark's pioneering rides of the massive waves at Northern California's Maverick's surf spot are well-known and well-documented. For nearly 15 years, he was unable to convince anyone to join him to ride those waves during the winter swell. But what is less well-known about him is his lifelong passion for design and innovation. Since age eight, he has dabbled in shaping surfboards. As he grew older and surfed other locations and larger waves, his designs evolved with each new challenge and opportunity. He experimented with new materials, designed fins for Big Waves, and explored using from one to four fins depending on conditions. Most recently he has turned his attention to new designs for safety vests and standup paddleboards for use in big wave conditions.

His experience with water safety teams and what he learned from his own array of horrendous wipeouts (plus the ban on Jet Skis in the waters of Maverick's except on the day of the contest) led Clark to spend nearly 10 years developing prototypes for inflatable vests to help surfers who get "rag-dolled" by a huge wave, and whose best option was to "climb the leash" to their "tombstoning" buoyant surfboard in order to find their way to the surface more quickly. The vest is operated by the surfer and reduces the need for support boats or Jet Skis. Teaming up with Quatic™, Clark recently introduced an inflatable neoprene surf vest, "a flotation device designed for the demands of Big Waves," says Clark. "Because it was developed and tested by surfers, the design of the vest gives the user complete control and flexibility in all climates and conditions."[3]

Clark tested and added several features over time via input from surfers, stand-up paddleboarders, and other watermen and waterwomen. "Ultimately, testing prototypes at Maverick's—one of the most extreme surfing destinations in the world—allowed us to hone in on a final design."[4] Among the options of the vest are: an instant, manual ripcord; a separate deflation cord to manage buoyancy; a second ripcord for more extreme conditions; and an oral inflation tube, much like those found on airplane safety vests.

"Because rough water and extreme waves may lead to emergency situations where less buoyancy can be an advantage, the vest also lets you regulate your flotation. Once deployed, releasing some pressure can assist in avoiding impact, curbing speed, or simply regaining control. Afterward, re-inflation while still in the water is as simple as pulling the second ripcord when the danger has minimized or when fatigue sets in."[5]

The advances in life vests are the latest in a series of breakthrough developments that goes back to the creation of the modern wetsuit. Few equipment innovations contributed to the rise of surfing worldwide and year round than the wetsuit. In the 1940s, San Francisco surfer Jack O'Neill was braving the cold water and high wind conditions at San Francisco's Ocean Beach. The ever-ingenious O'Neill and the diehard surfers of that era would often be seen wearing wool sweaters into the water for warmth and wind protection. Then one day O'Neill had a daring idea: a full bodysuit made of plastic foam.

O'Neill experimented with various designs and materials, putting his expertise as a journeyman draftsman to good use. "I knew from my physics classes that air was a good insulator. It worked good, except it didn't have tensile strength, so I had to take it and put plastic on the outside."[6] Several iterations and years later, in 1952, his friend and fellow surfer Harry Hind told him about a new chemical product. "He saw what I was trying to do . . . and he says, 'Hey, try this neoprene.' It really worked well."[7]

O'Neill and his large family headed to Santa Cruz, CA.[8] There were more surfers there and O'Neill wetsuits sold well from his surf shop at Cowell Beach. As so often happens, the O'Neill Surf Shop quickly became the main hub of Santa Cruz surfing activity. In those days, surfers had a bad reputation in town. "When I first came to Santa Cruz, surfing was a dirty word," explains O'Neill. "They thought we were a bunch of druggies, that we didn't work."[9]

Over the next decade the stereotype changed dramatically, so much so that Santa Cruz now calls itself "Surf City USA." So, in a 10-year span a *city* changed its identity, and the world of surfing had a game-changing shift.

WATCH THE WAVE BUILD

For more than a century, philosophers, business analysts and scientists have been using waves as a metaphor for cycles and changing conditions. In all cases, the prevailing theme is that things change in waves and cycles. A set rolls in, with a seemingly harmless adjustment or iteration. The utility of the new iteration grows and expands until it hits Big Wave status, and is capable of wiping out the prior way of thinking and doing things.

According to a recent BizShifts article, "Nobody creates a wave. It just 'happens' out of countless uncontrollable interactions of the sea with winds, the movement of the moon, and anything else that affects bodies of water. Surfers don't create waves . . . A wave is just a wave and no more. It may be small, medium, large, or a 'tube.' It may be good for surfing or not. The wave, as a generative metaphor, symbolizes the will of a social context to direct its resources/energy towards a sector or product (goods or services). The 'sea,' in this metaphor represents human beings, a society; and, incredible as it may seem, society is as uncontrollable as the wave . . ."[10]

According to brand identity specialist and blogger David Brier, ". . . the major difference between the innovator and the ordinary person [is that] innovators saw the dots and connected them, while others 1) didn't see them, or 2) if they did, they didn't explore, question, or connect any of them . . . It's a constant attentiveness to how things are applied . . . it's the foundation for innovation. So what is innovation? It's those other dots; the ones others miss . . . and, having the certainty to know that the dots you see are not only valid, but necessary if the world is to move forward . . ."[11]

I have been arguing much the same thing throughout this book: the Big Wave surfer is the model innovator, one who incessantly connects many "dots" . . . in an instant. From learning to swim and paddle, to looking "outside," to overcoming fear of wiping out, to knowing specific ocean conditions—all of this is processed instantly from wave to wave. Before making a big move on a Big Wave there are hundreds of data points going through the surfer's head. Add to this the changing conditions once they commit to ride a specific wave, and you get a sense of the complexity of the endeavor and the inventiveness of the surfer.

In my ongoing 25-year research on innovators, the data shows that few things are more important than the ability to connect dots. More specifically, innovators connect dots in unique ways and can see those dots forming pictures long before others do. They see a whole, new "picture" sooner and more clearly. To do this requires being willing and able to let go of the pre-existing ways of doing things in order to explore other options, veer off the beaten path, and make change your ally.

NO DARE, NO FLARE

As Jeff Bezos, the founder of Amazon says, "In business, what's dangerous is not to evolve."[12] No one understood this better than Steve Jobs. As mentioned, when working in collaboration with designer Jony Ive, Jobs was a self-described perfectionist, always looking to simplify a design and make it intuitively viable. He never settled for mediocrity. He understood that designers and engineers know more about making things that are "different" than they do about making things that are "better." So he always pushed for greater simplicity of design and intuitive ease of use. He also knew that nothing is ever truly perfect, yet you must always aim in that direction. He was the poster child for "Dare Big!"

"Everything we make I could describe as being partially wrong, because it's not perfect," said Ive, describing the wave of public complaints that come with every new product. "We get to do it again. That's one of the things Steve and I used to talk about: 'Isn't this fantastic? Everything we aren't happy about . . . we can try and fix.'"[13]

To the Big Wave surfer, "try and then fix" is the name of the game if the goal is to take smart risks on XL waves. As I heard a surfer say at The Wedge in Southern California a long time ago, "No dare, no flare." And as Mark Matthews texted his buddies from his hospital bed after he dislocated his shoulder at the legendary December 6, 2015 big wave competition at Pe'ahi, "Stay safe, but not too safe."

In Big Wave surfing, where your life is literally on the line with each wave, you cannot afford to rest on your laurels or how you performed on the wave. If you do, the next wave may *be* your last. So you have to be smart, *very* smart, and take calculated risks, not random chances.

Shaun Tomson says, "Youth is a time for being impulsive and taking risks, but it has to be tempered with caution. Life is so precious. Sure, risk can heighten that experience, but you have to be careful."[14] Raised in the tradition of surfing nobility, his childhood hero was none other than two-time Olympic Gold medal swim champion Duke Kahanamoku. Tomson says, "I think I always saw the sporting component of surfing differently than most. Duke Kahanamoku was my father's hero and he was my hero. We loved the nobility associated with surfing . . . My father always taught me to win like a gentleman and lose like a man."[15]

Tomson still pushes his own limits, but in a *smart* way. "The stoke and the satisfaction I got at 59 years old is the same as when I was 19. Performance becomes relative to yourself and not to anyone else," he says. "The push for me is to be as good as I can be. Maybe not better than I was, but as good as I can be on each wave."[16]

Daring big knows no age limit. And as trailblazer Dave Kalama has said, Big Wave surfers have to have half a screw loose and a healthy sense of denial! That's why in the surfing world, the Big Wave surfers are almost heroic figures.

World champion Stephanie Gilmore understands about grace under fire. She knows that many of her opportunities come as a result of women who pioneered before her. "I've always loved Lisa Andersen, because while she was at the top of the field [four world titles], she kept beauty and grace in her surfing style. She never tried to surf 'like the boys,' she continued perfecting her own approach and her style is timeless because of that," says Gilmore. To Gilmore, Lisa Andersen was powerful because she had her own personal style and stayed "feminine." "She led the way for us young tomboys to follow suit. I also love Keila 'Sister' Moniz. Watching her ride a longboard is majestic. It can be compared to watching ballet. Her moves are refined but groovy and so stylish."

The "risks" for a female Big Wave surfer can increase when trying too hard to be one of the boys. All the women want is equal opportunity and contest parity with the guys. "Whenever we [girls] get together and surf big waves there's a really cool energy and the level of surfing gets raised every time . . . So this year our goal is to show up at the men's events and surf before and after them. Just to show the contest organizers that we can do it too," says Gilmore.

The objective then is to be Women Who Ride Giants. Simple as that. "People see men charging Big Waves, and they think 'Oh, those guys are nuts.' Then they see women surf Big Waves, and their minds bend," says Gilmore.

And how did the men in the lineup react? "They're super-nice to almost everyone out there. At the same time, you have to prove yourself. Nobody's going to say 'It's your turn, go.' If you want the wave and you're the one in position, the only way you're going to get it is if you put your head down and paddle."[17]

As Maya Gabeira told me, Big Wave surfing is still a macho endeavor. But to her, though boys will be boys, girls needn't be boys too. "You don't want to make choices that lead to your early death," Maya said. "But I don't think it's in me to stop because I could die. I know that nobody does as much work as I do if they don't want it really bad. I know that I want it really bad."[18]

Echoing her comments are those of Big Wave legend Dave Kalama. While acting as a commentator at what many think of as the biggest waves ever paddled into in a competition, December 6, 2015 at Pe'ahi (aka "Jaws"), Maui, Kalama said that these athletes have a level of risk and commitment unlike, for example, a professional basketball or soccer player who knows for sure that win or lose they will be going out to dinner after a game. If Big Wave surfers have a bad day there's no certainty they're going to make it home alive.

"That makes us desire it more. That's where it started for me. Being told I can't do things because I'm a girl," says Keala Kennelly. Having two brothers and a strong dad, she grew up hearing that some things were not for girls. "There's nothing more frustrating than knowing that you have a gift that sets you apart and not being able to utilize it.

"As every yin must have its yang, Teahupo'o also became the place of some of my worst nightmares. First time I went there I almost died. I was so excited to ride that beautiful wave that I didn't realize how actually big it was that day." She got caught inside, her board breaking into three pieces, and was pounded face first into the coral reef by the wave until she couldn't move. "I was held down for two waves, saw my life flash before my eyes, and I thought, 'Man this is it!'

"I felt so defeated in that moment that I felt maybe I have reached my limit because I'm a girl." Introspective by nature, this moment provided her with an opportunity to face her fears and her limits. "Just as I was about to give up, I found the strength in my life and was able to save myself. I returned to Teahupo'o every year for many years . . . but it took me many years before I found the courage to ride it again at that massive size," she says. "If I could just get over my fear of what did happen and what could happen, I knew I could get the ride of my life." So she decided to go back and face her fears and find the next Big Wave. She talked one of the local guys in to giving her a tow in. Up to then, no one thought a woman could ride a wave of that size at that break. "I proved first to myself and then to the rest of the world that, yes, it is possible."

Ever the realist, she says, "People think that because I like to ride these massive, life-threatening waves that I have no fear. Nothing could be further from the truth. I am terrified of this wave. This wave has almost killed me . . . I've had horrific injuries from this wave, some that have scarred me for life. So why do I do it? Why do I keep going back and putting my life in danger? Sometimes I ponder that question in my own head and the answer always speaks to me loud and clear.

"There'll be forever a gnawing at your soul telling you there is something more. That wave haunts me . . . but it also seduces me, because that wave offers a heightened feeling of being alive. That feeling I am truly addicted to. My desire to feel that becomes stronger than the fear."[19] She paddles back out because she has had a taste of something deep inside her that is so valuable that she can't *not* do it.

DON'T FEAR THE BIG BETS

Kevin Weil, SVP of product at Twitter, was recently asked who outside the tech domain inspires him. "I think the work that Elon Musk is doing is incredible—the way he takes big bets and inspires people to go after really, really big goals. People tell him that things are impossible and he builds anyway, from PayPal, to Tesla, to Space X. So I love how he approaches problems and he doesn't back down."[20] For example, the critics and skeptics came out of the woodwork when Musk announced his plan to build a new kind of car, the Tesla. The naysayers also had a field day when he revealed the car would be battery powered, and that there would be no traditional dealerships. The most successful entrepreneurs are sometimes the ones who dare the biggest and overcome their fears the fastest.

Shaun Tomson learned the importance of daring big on the biggest of stages: Hawaii's North Shore. "My first Big Wave—paddle, paddle, paddle—I was really determined to go. So from a physical perspective, how do you break fear? What did I do differently? I took three more strokes. And I went over the edge. And then I'm riding. That board just put me into the wave perfectly. And I did a bottom turn. And when I came out of it, people were laughing at me and 'The Pink Banana' board I was using.

"From an entrepreneurial perspective, you've gotta make that commitment to do it, and do it even harder. You have to go, and you go even harder. And when you go, and you go harder, you break through and the risk dissipates," he says. "It's an important concept, that if you go and go even harder, the fear dissipates and the risk factor diminishes. Its funny, I'm asked often, 'What's your approach in surfing?' I say there's three approaches: attack, attack, attack! As soon as you're defensive, you're finished." Then he adds, "[Attacking] creates a stillness, a calmness. I watch a lot of sports. And the defensive guy is going to lose, and he's going to get hurt. The attacking guy is usually the winner. Like the surfer who has a big wipeout and comes up smiling."

Hawaiian surfer Pancho Sullivan stayed away from the pro circuit until he was 32, preferring the life of free surfing to the grind of the pro-surfing tour. But as with entrepreneurs and innovators, there sometimes comes a moment for surfers when crucial decisions must be made. At times those decisions are calculated and logical, at other times pure muscle memory of past successes kicks in.

My mother used to say, "Your life can change in an afternoon." One afternoon, Pancho made a decision that changed his life. "I felt like I came to another crossroads and was ready for a different kind of challenge, so I just dove in. That's been a recurring theme in my life," he says. "At one point, when I was younger, I had just sold a few boards to pay for rent, and when I was driving home I just happened to stop off at the World Cup of Surfing contest at Sunset Beach. They were accepting beach entries, so I took my rent money and on a whim beach-entered the contest, made the main-event rounds, and that laid the tracks to a career in pro surfing."[21]

You too can dare big . . . this afternoon.

SURFER STEP
8

DARE BIG

Endemic to Big Wave surfers and innovators is pushing boundaries and facing fears. Big Wave surfing is relatively new, propelled by advances in training, board shaping and materials, fin designs, and Jet Skis. In recent years, extra safety equipment has been developed, including quick-release leashes and inflatable vests. These innovations help Big Wave surfers find new challenges, new locations, and try new maneuvers. But perhaps more important is the mental preparation, the Mindset that fosters courage and confidence in the face of obstacles and barriers.

South African surfer Chris Bertish won the 2010 Maverick's contest after barely arriving on time from a frantic, 36-hour trip from his homeland. "Courage hardly sums it up," he says of Maverick's. "You have to be completely motivated to overcome your fears, especially when everyone is telling you not to do it."[22]

Entrepreneurs have that same drive. The energy of the endeavor and the belief in it pushes them and keeps them going forward when others would pull back. The entrepreneur, as the surfer, quickly learns to take smart risks, to dare big.

Twitter co-founder Biz Stone sees opportunity in the face of adversity. "Creativity comes from constraints. If you give an artist unlimited rein and budget, there's too much going on," he says. "But if you have some kind of constraints around it, the human mind is forced to get more creative. It's just the way we're wired. We come up with really creative solutions when our backs are against the wall." So just as a surfer has to adjust to the potential and the limitations of every wave, so too does the entrepreneur.

And when asked what he thought of "stability and security" he says, "I don't think they existed in my brain. I jokingly referred to my future self as the guy who would take care of all the problems I was creating. I lived off my credit card and paid my rent with it. I racked up so much debt that I calculated it would take me over 200 years to pay it back if I paid the minimum each month," he said. "I thought 'Future Biz' would work it all out. He would be smarter and would fix all that stuff. I like that guy. He totally fixed it all."[23]

THINGS TO DO:

If you feel trepidation or are fearful about your idea, especially if your idea is bold and audacious, think of a prior accomplishment and try this:

1. Make three columns on a piece of paper or on an electronic device.

2. Label the first two columns 1. *Big Idea*. 2. *Big Risks*.

3. Fill in each column as completely as possible. Describe the idea you had in some detail. Then chronicle the risks that had accompanied the idea.

4. Review your replies.

5. Label column three: *Big Actions*. In the third column describe the *Big Actions* that you used to counter the *Big Risk* in order to achieve the *Big Idea*.

6. Re-read the page in its entirety from right to left, i.e., from column three to column one. This serves the purpose of showing how what you did affected what you *thought*.

When times get tough, re-read your accounts of past victories.

9

NEVER
SURF
ALONE

"**W**HEN YOU'RE JOCKEYING FOR SMALL WAVES, THAT'S ALL ego. But when you're in a big-wave situation just trying to survive, it's totally different," says Nate Fletcher. "If someone gets a good [big] wave, I'm just screaming for them. You want to see everyone charge hard and do great things. Afterwards it just feels like this big exhale, and as long as everyone made it back safe, you're stoked. I think that's where the camaraderie comes from in Big-Wave surfing."[1]

Surfing is all about community and company. "Never surf alone" is a phrase you hear all the time in the world of Big Wave surfing, a phrase that may seem illogical at first for such a solitary sport. It's a phrase that has myriad meanings, some that are very subtle, even counterintuitive. The nuances are extensive because ironically, there are moments and situations when what

you do in the water you do totally alone. Like being an entrepreneur, Big Wave surfing can be a very isolating experience.
When you commit and put your head down to go over the
ledge of a 40-footer, at that moment you couldn't be more
alone. When you are held under for one or two or three more
waves, spanning two or three or five minutes, you are on your
own, as well.

You are also literally alone when you cannot get anyone to
go out into huge swells with you. Much like the budding entrepreneur working alone at nights in her home office, consider
the case of Jeff Clark, who as you have read earlier surfed
Maverick's by himself for nearly *15 years*, from 1975 to 1989!
"For [those] years Clark was the only person to ride the 'too
dangerous for surfing' waves off Pillar Point . . . His solitary
period at Maverick's is a stunning, unmatchable Big Wave
achievement," says my favorite surf historian Matt Warshaw.[2]
"He's a nut, really; he's psycho," says Santa Cruz's Josh Loya.
"Riding that place for all those years . . . God, I would *never*
do that. I wouldn't surf out there even *once* by myself."[3] In
truth, though, for all those years Clark challenged the mountainous waves solo, on the biggest days whenever possible he
had buddies like Brian Pinoche watching from the shore break
or the beach cliffs. Upon trying to convince Pinoche to go out
with him the first time anyone had attempted to ride Maverick's
on a big day, Clark, armed with only a 7'3" board recalls that
Pinoche, " . . . said something like, 'Good luck, and I'll call the
Coast Guard and tell 'em where I last saw you. But I'm not
going in.'"[4]

Frustrated that he could not get anyone local to go with him,
Clark drove north to San Francisco's Ocean Beach where he
was able to persuade Tom Powers and Dave Schmidt to check
out this secret spot not far away. "He blew us away that day,"
says Powers. "He was taking off super deep, charging into these

big, black, hideous pits. We were worried about him. We were awestruck."[5] Eighteen months later, *Surfer* magazine did a long story on Maverick's and Clark, and the whole world was equally and suddenly awestruck.

Ever philosophical, Clark says, "The Maverick's reef break out in the ocean existed long before I came along and will exist long after I am gone. The wave exists despite us, and Mother Nature has been good enough to let some of us use it as a playground when she sees fit, and has denied us at her whim," says Clark. "It was my personal surf spot for a very long time, but it's not my wave—*it was my sanctuary*. You have no idea the excitement I felt the first time I convinced someone to go out and surf it with me . . . As time wore on it became the destination of some of the world's best surfers. It was about the surfers and the stoke. It had a humble beginning."[6]

From those humble beginnings has come worldwide attention to some of the biggest waves on the planet, and an invitational contest held when Mother Nature deems it possible. According to Clark, the Titans of Maverick's contest has evolved and become a bit more professional by working with Cartel Management Inc., in collaboration with a group of five surfers, known as "Committee 5," who discuss and make recommendations on everything from the conditions, to selecting the competitors, to deciding when to hold the event. "It's a combination of guys who surf Maverick's, competitors, and people who know what happens in the water. The committee helps the event leadership focus on everything else related to the business and operations, and takes our recommendations for all things related to water. That lets each of us do what we know best." Clark doesn't run the contest, but acts as a technical adviser and board member. "And I'm quite happy about that. It is best run by people who understand not just how to run the business, but also how to put together a good team and treat people well."[7]

So it seems that if "it takes a village" to raise a child, "it takes a committee of five" to run a world-class competition. In business, there are also opportunities that will flourish if collaboration is fostered. The lone, do-it-all-myself entrepreneur is rare, and rightly so. It takes a team comprised of people with differing strengths to take most projects through to completion in a timely manner.

DRIVEN TO THIS LEVEL

To "never surf alone" is another way to push yourself beyond your limits. Often when you prepare and train, you are doing so by yourself. Yet even with the understanding that on one level you ultimately always surf "alone," to never truly surf alone is an accepted practice for XL surfers. From personal trainers to safety patrols, it's a collaborative support system to a solitary endeavour that can push you to new heights. There are layers of trust, collaboration, and camaraderie that surfing can model for entrepreneurs and company "cultures." "The reason I'm able to do what I do is because I have partners. I'm only arriving at this level because I'm being driven by these guys *to* this level," says Laird Hamilton.[8]

Bruce Irons grew up in Kauai with a tough group of friends who pushed him to surf better. He was teased, yelled at, and hassled. "It's just words. Inside you know what's right and what's wrong . . . With friends, that's when I get amped."[9] Having a brother who was among the world's best surfers also helped Bruce. When asked if either he or his brother would have been as good if they didn't have each other, he said, "I don't think so . . . I wouldn't be where I'm at if it wasn't for him . . . We're trying to outdo each other but we're also trying to get a compliment from each other."[10]

"I'm just trying to go bigger and better . . . and look cool doing it," he says. Partners can come from near and far. For example, there is no question the surfing community has benefitted from advances in the world of skateboarding. Aerials and cut backs have added a special flare to performance surfing, and even the angles of cut backs in Big Wave surfing. "Never surf alone" extends to being kept company by your heroes, past and present, and by knowledge of what they can do on a board.

Though Matt Meola is not known primarily as a Big Wave surfer, he is among the best "big air" surfers on smaller waves. Meola has been a friend and admirer of another big air great, Kelly Slater. For many years the challenge of aerialists was to do a 360-degree spin without grabbing the side of the board in the air. Over time, several accomplished that and the bar was then raised to a 540—one and one-half revolutions.

Slater was the first to do a 540, using a double grab in the process. Then, in May 2015, footage went viral documenting Meola's 540 *with a flip*. "It felt good to do the move. I guess it's cool that I landed it first, but if he woulda pulled it I woulda been super stoked for him. I don't know. I'm not that competitive. I like to see my friends rip and do new stuff."[11]

Was this the best air that's ever been done? "I'd like to think so . . . I mean Kelly's air was really sick but . . . when Kelly did his 540 I was like, 'Oh, man,' 'cause I was trying that air for so long. But then it was like, well, the only way to better it is to do something like that with a flip, or get upside-down or something. I don't know, I'd like to think it was one of the best airs done. That's what Albee [Layer] and John John [Florence] told me."[12]

In the modern era of Big Wave surfing, it's important to have a partner—to be part of a pair who are well-matched at every level. You each can operate as an extra pair of eyes, drive the Jet Ski into harm's way to rescue someone if need be, and keep the equipment and the surfer safe and sound. "Every time I surf

Maverick's, I have a personal lifeguard, Chris Killen, on a ski, watching every wave," says Santa Cruz-based Big Wave surfer Ken "Skindog" Collins.[13] Some surfers I have talked to have gone so far as to say that if you can't find anyone to partner with, it's irresponsible to yourself and your family to go out solo.

In the relatively small Big Wave surfing community there is an especially strong bond, in part because of the shared understanding of the serious risks. Everyone is in The Big Peril Club, so everyone looks out for one another. "If you are surfing with a buddy and you don't see him, you go looking for him," says Mark Healey.[14] Says surf historian Matt Warshaw, "Because there aren't many Big-Wave surfers, and because they make a point of looking out for each other during heavy conditions, the intergroup bonds tend to be very strong." Says Flea Virostky, "When somebody eats it out there, I'll be waiting to see if he comes up, if he needs help, or whatever . . . Even if it's just some kook."[15]

With the advent of social media and cell phone cameras, in an instant the world will know about a major swell being ridden or a life-threatening wipeout. When Maya Gabeira had her gut-wrenching wipeout at Nazaré, Portugal, hours later fellow surfer and World Champion Shaun Tomson saw the video and sent her an email with suggestions about a new protective vest.

He shared the email with me, in which he offered her suggestions about who to contact to get state-of-the-art safety equipment. Maya's reply was typical of the mutual respect among these athletes: "What happened shall never happen again, that was a sequence of mistakes or lack of safety that we still face in our sport, but as a team we are aware now that we can't take another chance like that. We will work to improve. Again, I am so honored to have received your email. Sometimes support and direction is all an athlete needs to take it to the next level. I will continue to work in that direction."[16]

Nazaré, Portugal, has become a testing ground for both equipment and partnerships. I've mentioned several such partnerships already in this book, including Maya Gabeira and Carlos Burlé. Recently a group of eight surfers including Andrew Cotton, Tom Butler, Kealii Mamala, Cliff and Will Skudin, António Silva, Rodrigo Koxa, and Sebastian Steudtner organized together in preparation for a Nazaré swell.

In January 2014, a massive storm in the North Atlantic named Hercules produced super waves that hit the shores of Southern Europe with such power it was named "The Black Swell." With adrenaline pumping in their veins, innovative equipment ready to use, and their support teams in place, the Praia do Norte line up formed. Paddling in was impossible due to wave speed, so Jet Skis were mandatory: "You need them to save lives, and to tow riders into the fast-moving giants. Surfers became rescuers; rescuers became surfers. All with a common goal: to excel at their jobs," wrote surfertoday.com.[17]

"I've just surfed the biggest wave of my life," wrote Steudtner, the German charger. "This morning, I went the fastest I ever have on a surfboard riding down this lump of blue," added Butler. Conditions were ideal, from wave height to wind direction to tides. "It was one of the best moments of my life. It was one of the most special moments that I could ever live in the surf! I had never seen waves so big and so strong. I can't wait to surf another day like this," concluded Koxa.

"Nazaré gets pretty dangerous. It's not like most Big Wave spots where it's organized or goes into a channel. It's like a beach break that's all over the place. So safety and communication are key. It's the only place I surf with a radio," said Andrew Cotton.[18]

Waves were recorded at nearly 80 feet. Wave speed was calculated at 50-plus miles per hour. In such monstrous conditions, it's obvious that you should never surf alone. In fact, in such conditions you never surf without a *team*. When the stakes are that high, communication, trust, planning, and collaboration are the name of the game—a lesson every entrepreneur and startup can learn from. Though there were eight surfers in the treacherous waters, dozens more were in the water and ready to help at a moment's notice.

But, to "never surf alone" is not just about safety and equipment. The human element actually reigns supreme. Having fun matters, so having someone to talk to, and to travel and laugh with make for special moments and lasting memories.

TALK STORY

Among the oldest and most endearing of traditions in the surfing community is the Hawaiian "talk story." Arising out of an oral culture long before the arrival of Captain Cook, traditionally talk story was local and personal. According to surf historian Patrick Moser, before Cook, Hawaiians would talk story in the Hawaiian language.

Using Hawaiian "pidgin" language (a mix of many languages that workers used to communicate with their plantation bosses) is a more recent development. Stories are passed down from generation to generation, keeping history and lore alive.

With the arrival of Cook in the Hawaiian Islands in the 1700s, talk story began a gradual change. Hawaiians learned to read, write, and speak "proper" English and were no longer totally dependent on the oral tradition. But with literacy came a price. Much of what was not written down after the 1700s has been lost until as recently as the so-called Hawaiian Renaissance in the 1970s. The Hawaiian Renaissance returned pidgin to prominence, and since then talk story has flourished.

Similarly, in the surfing community a version of talk story is shared among friends on road trips, on front porches and evenings on beaches, and most recently via video and audio clips that move instantaneously around the planet. The Big Wave community is especially tight-knit. The common bond formed by the long preparation, high risk, and all-consuming passion they share takes "never surf alone" to exponential levels.

Nic Lamb added a cautionary note in my conversation with him. I asked him what he thinks of the saying, "Never surf alone."

"I love being alone. I surf alone often. Is it safe? Probably not. But I don't always need to be around people to be satisfied. I love reflecting on my own, kinda self-auditing. In business though, when you're trying to start something up you have to be constantly networking."[19] but it pales in comparison to the Big Wave surf community. "(Big Wave) surfing's a situation where you're fearful, where you're aware that life is short," says surf legend Tom Curren, "but where you're reminded that only God knows how long you've got. You experience fear and faith at the same time."

FINDING GRACE

Like Tom Curren, Stephanie Gilmore is among the most respected surfers in the world. She pays attention to her peers for insights into the development of a "style." Wise beyond her years, she offers sound advice and perspective useful to any entrepreneur: "Style is found in calmness, joy, the fine details of body language, spontaneity, aggression (sometimes), and flow. It's a most pleasurable show when these ingredients all come together," she says. "I love to watch Tom Curren, Kelia Moniz, Rob Machado, Joel Parkinson, Mason Ho, Alex Knost, Dave Rastovich, and Dane Reynolds. They're all true performance artists, and it's magic when they ride a wave." How many entrepreneurs out there have an equivalent sense of business history and/or know who the role models are?

Then she adds something very insightful, something that my many years of research and experience with entrepreneurs and innovators support: "The most stylish people are born with the ability to not overthink, and to operate on feeling. When it comes to style, intuition is powerful, but I think style can be worked on—to a degree," she says. "Things like hand placement, posture, and where lines are drawn on a wave face can all be improved. But when feeling takes precedence over thought, the style that results is your own unique approach. I try to make slight changes in my stance so that I can have better structure—and therefore more strength—when trying high-performance maneuvers.

"I love when assertion collides with femininity and becomes grace," she says. "Insert good waves, and everyone wins."[21] And by the way, Stephanie is six-time world champion. She's got style to spare and to share.

For the entrepreneur and the innovator, the name of the game is often playing between the notes, improvising, iterating, orchestrating what's *not* been there before, and finding your own style. Style comes from allowing feelings and intuition into the mix. Isn't that what a good brand is all about—creating a feeling about it that makes you trust it and want to buy it and stay stoked about it?

SURFER STEP

9

NEVER SURF ALONE

Like many sports, surfing is solitary in a way, but can be
enhanced by having companions with you—having others to

travel and paddle with adds to the fun and encourages you to perfect new moves and surf spots. And, of course, surfing with friends enhances your safety. From teaching each other new tricks to "talking story" to making a leash tourniquet after a cut on a low-lying reef, collaboration is king in the Big Wave world.

The history of entrepreneurship too is replete with dynamic duos that at first may seem odd couplings. Steve Jobs and Steve Wozniak, Larry Page and Sergey Brin. Bill Gates and Paul Allen. Each duo had complementary strengths. Each could not have created what they did alone.

Sometimes the pairing takes the form of the customer and the product developer working together to create something unique. Sydney-based 3D-printed surfboard maker Disrupt Surfing is taking "never surf alone" seriously with its totally customized boards designed by the end user via a new app. With the rise of surfing worldwide, demand for quality boards is ever increasing. "You're getting more and more expats following their careers but still wanting to surf; you get tourists to places like Hainan Island in China, and also locals because the culture's starting to change and people are getting in the water," says Founder and CEO Gary Elphick. Adds Annabel Madushan, one of his new distribution partners and founder of Sri Lanka-based Surf Arugam, "Surfing is a growing trend in Sri Lanka. For our customers to be able to design something from scratch that suits their taste and for us to not have to go through four layers of distributors is really appealing."[22]

In my research, few entrepreneurs build a successful business solo. From ideation, to "proof of concept," to execution, enlisting others in the endeavor is a valuable investment of time and money. To innovators, building on your strengths and collaborating with others whose strengths complement your own is a common and productive strategy. And remember, strange bedfellows make great partners. In the marketplace, as in the ocean, surrounding yourself with others different from you whom you trust and respect can re-energize your passion through good and tough times. New perspectives enable you to "stay stoked."

THINGS TO DO:

Collaboration is crucial to success. Complete the following:

1. Make a list of your *Top 10 Strengths*, starting with your strongest.

2. Show your list to five trusted friends and/or colleagues and ask them to rank your top 10 as they see you, from strongest to weakest. You may be surprised at how they view you.

3. Tally their feedback and start a new, *inverted* list with your weakest rated items on top.

4. Beside each of those 10 items, write the name of someone you know whose strengths would complement your weaknesses.

5. Keep this list handy, and revise it often. When you hit an impasse in one of the areas, contact the person you have identified as strong in that area for help and guidance.

10
STAY
STOKED!

IN JUST ABOUT ANY CONVERSATION WITH SURFERS, "STOKED" is a term that will appear multiple times. It is used as a noun ("I crave the stoke") or a verb ("I am so stoked") or an adverb ("I'm living the stoked life"). Being stoked is the epitome of living. When someone is stoked, there is no limit to what he or she can do.

Clearly, *being* stoked is directly related to passion and *staying* stoked is an aspirational goal for surfer and entrepreneur alike. An MBA student recently asked me, "In all your work with entrepreneurs and CEOs, what have they regretted the most?" I had to think hard, but upon reflection my reply came with conviction. "There are two main regrets I have witnessed. The first is not being able to make decisions in a timely manner. And the second is not trusting their 'gut'." Intuition, hunches, and passion play a bigger role in business success than you might assume.

Passion takes energy, and sustaining one's passions is the name of the game for the entrepreneur and innovator, just as it is for the Big Wave surfers of the world. When passion wanes, the energy of the endeavor declines. Conversely, when the stoke is "on," it can last a lifetime.

For Joel Tudor, the stoke is in the family DNA passed on from generation to generation. "My dad surfs pretty much every day and he always has. It's just what we do. I've never known any other way. I had an opportunity to play team sports at one point, and I remember my dad saying, 'Oh, you want to play team sports? That's cool. Your mom can take you to do that, 'cause I'm going surfing.' And I thank him for that," he says. "That's what my dad did with me, and that's what I do with my kids. For me to be happy, surfing has to be the center of my existence. You can have all these other things that people pursue, but at the end of everything, you're taking a dirt nap."[1]

Dorian "Doc" Paskowitz, surfing's soul-searching philosopher, took his "dirt nap" in 2014 at the age of 93. "Doc" was a role model for generations of kids who passed through his surf camps and listened attentively to his accrued wisdom. He reflected on his passion in 2010 for *Surfer* magazine. "Whatever surfers are getting right, they're getting it from their time in the water. Whatever they're getting wrong happens out of the water. The landward side of the beach, for all time, has been the more dangerous place, more dangerous than the water." He added, "Great enterprises all begin with one guy saying to himself, 'Oh, I could do that . . .' One thing all surfers have in common, if they're in love with surfing, then they're in love with the sea; and if they're in love with the sea, then they're in love with God. That's what makes surfing so magical . . ."[2]

Near the end of his life Doc was getting frail and going blind, but the stoke was as strong as ever. "Recently I paddled out at Waikiki. I can't see anymore, so I catch waves by listening to the waves crash, the people laughing and having fun, and by feeling the ocean moving beneath me. We are all smaller than the sea, and bigger than ourselves when we ride the waves."[3]

Hanging above the desk of Shaun Tomson is a well-known poem by William Butler Yeats, "An Irish Airman Foresees His Death." When he reads its lines he gets "the sensation of flight, like the airman in the poem; the breath of the wave; the sense of danger; the commitment to fly in the face of that danger; and the importance of balance and imagination."[4] At the end of the day, Tomson decides to "live in the moment and to choose one path and follow wherever it takes me. That path is not a destination, which surfers are never concerned with while on a wave, but simply living with passion . . . what Yeats terms 'a lonely impulse of delight.' In the end I followed my passion."[5]

Jeff Clark's "lonely impulse of delight" has been well-chronicled here and elsewhere. His passions skyrocketed at the moment he committed to take the wave. "My heart was in my throat . . . the sound was deafening, and the vibration of the explosion rumbled through my body. I could finally feel the sheer power of this wave, and it was shocking. I recalibrated my lineups, I studied the waves, and I pulled myself closer to the break zone. Now it was time."

He waited for the right, first wave. "It came, and I turned and committed . . . I felt the wave lift me and I dug harder, head down, driving down this mass of water that was lifting past me. Finally it let me go down the face with the release of a free-fall. I snapped to my feet, going straight down this watery mountain. It was a gray day but I will never forget the dark shadow of my first wave." Then, for 15 years he had this wave to himself, as no one would take him up on his offer to share Maverick's. As he says, "Just me and the ocean." Then he adds, "It's been more than 35 years since I first paddled out at Maverick's. I still surf there . . . And I'm still stoked."[6]

"The majority of guys who are doing it and doing it well, they're the ones that are doing it because they love it, "says Greg Long. "Why do [we] do this? We love it. It means something to a lot of us," echoes Ken "Skindog" Collins. "Don't take things too seriously," says Jordy Smith. "Surfing is the greatest sport and lifestyle in the world, and the best surfer in the water is the one having the most fun." Restating the obvious, Greg Long says "We all see and think relatively the same."[7]

Six-time world champion Stephanie Gilmore has found aesthetic guidance in surfing. "There's a beauty to balance. I believe balance is needed in all aspects of life to achieve greatness because to evolve and get better, we must always be learning. I believe we should always be open to new things and opportunities, appreciate your achievements but always envision a new adventure—that way we stay excited and will always take a fresh approach to whatever it is we're doing," she says. "Of course you need to be able to channel your focus at certain times to achieve in those moments, but having an open view to the bigger picture has always helped me to succeed."[8]

Surfing evokes passion, and the stoke among Big Wave surfers is universal. In the 20 years of research that ultimately led to this book, the dominant factor present is the unbounded enthusiasm for the sport and the lifestyle that goes with it. For many, surfing is both a physical and metaphysical endeavor. That's why Laird Hamilton can honestly say that to stop loving surfing is what "sin" would be to him.

In my long involvement in the entrepreneurial and innovation world, I can attest that if that level of passion for the material and the immaterial were present in the start-ups, the success rate would substantially increase. Too often the driving force of the endeavour is solely monetary. Too often impatience undermines progress. Too often a sense of financial entitlement overtakes the wisdom embedded in pure passion.

REAL DESIRE CAN'T BE BOUGHT

Keala Kennelly recently told her life story and some lessons she's learned from surfing Big Waves to a TedX Malibu audience. "I think in life we all fall victim of letting money and financial security stand in the way of what we truly desire. It causes us to make choices that aren't in line with what our heart is telling us to do. What would you be doing if money was no object," she asked. ". . . Everyday people do things that have no prize money check, no financial reward, but if what they are doing is making them come alive . . . the personal satisfaction from that is the reward," she says. "It's something money can't buy."[9]

Returning to the Big Waves and coral reef that ripped off the right side of her face took her years. But she knew she had to get back to that place and ride or else her fears would overtake her stoke and passion. "Real desire can't be bought, it comes from within. The way you fulfill your desire is not by investing in 'things' but by investing in yourself. By staying true to yourself, doing what you love, and most importantly not letting your gifts go to waste . . . I'm here to tell you, it's worth it!"[10]

So, the good news is that stoke is free! It won't cost you an enrollment fee. It won't be dolled out to a chosen few. And, it's there for the taking.

"Anytime you step into the ocean, you're in an environment that's completely uncontrolled by humans," says Mark Healey. "Everyone needs to connect with that sort of wildness in some way, especially in a time when there's so much noise and distraction in our daily lives."[11]

"Surfers know how to exist with very little," adds Ben Martin in an article entitled, "Why Surfers Make Great Entrepreneurs (And Vice Versa)." Surfers "can make $100 dollars last longer than most people would imagine possible. They don't go on holidays, they go on expeditions, and they want to stay away for as long as they possibly can. Two months on a remote Indonesian island eating nothing but rice and bananas? If the waves are good, it's all worth it. Surfers make sacrifices for their passion, just like the most successful startups."[12]

IT'S OKAY TO BE RAW . . . AND FLAWED

No discussion about surfers connecting with the beauty and the distractions in daily life can proceed without talking about the late Andy Irons. As I mentioned earlier, Andy Irons was the poster child for living fast and dying young. He passed away at age 32 of cardiac arrest, related to coronary artery disease and acute mixed drug ingestion. He was a reluctant role model for "charging" hard and challenging the status quo on his own terms. He died too young. His stoke for waves proved no match for his inner demons.

On the occasion of what would have been Andy's 37th birthday, Taylor Paul, writing for *SURFING Magazine*, spoke for most of the surfing community, saying, "What surfing loved most about Andy—more than the world titles and rivalries and Teahupo'o drops and Indo super sessions—was that he reminded us that it was okay to be human. To be raw. Passionate. Flawed. Complicated. To care and to claim and to punch and to hug and to cry tears of pain and tears of joy."[13]

At times fiercely competitive, at other times self-reflective to a fault, Andy Irons was surfing's Everyman and Everywoman. "That unfiltered humanity bled into his surfing and you couldn't help but feel something when you watched him. He would have been 37 today. He would have had a party. He would have gone surfing. He would have inspired us. He still does . . . Happy birthday, Andy."[14]

Robert Lambert is a young entrepreneur in Los Angeles with nearly as much stoke for business as he has for surfing—a regular guy and a passionate surfer. "I was spending a ton of time driving out to the 15 to 20 recurring business meetings I had each month with investors and entrepreneurs," Lambert said, "and it became frustrating."[15] A lifelong surfer, he saw the hours on the road eating into the hours he could spend chasing waves. After mentioning his concerns to his friends and colleagues, he was surprised and pleased to find out how many of them also surfed. Then came the light bulb: "Shoot, why don't we all meet up surfing? They loved it."[16]

The Silicon Beach Surfers Club was born and started growing immediately. "It started as just seven or so people in the industry that I knew could surf well," said Lambert. "But all of them brought three or four new people they knew, and before you knew it, we had 50 members." Highly organized compared to the norm of surf adventures, he launched a website, created an application process, scheduled paddle-outs for members three to four times a week, and began sending surf reports to all the members every morning.

The club's success is due to a focus on surfing above business, and because of its selective application process. The club accepts only around 30 percent of applicants. "We're looking for people who are either life-long surfers or who are looking to be life-long surfers," said Lambert. "So if someone who applies can't really surf, we send them for lessons. After a few months, if they prove they are capable surfers, they get put back in the application tunnel."[17]

"People always wonder how business and surf mix, because surf culture has always been pictured as very laid back while business culture is always pictured as the complete opposite," says Lambert. "But it's not like people are out on the waves talking business. The last thing anyone in a surf lineup wants to talk about is their job. It's about making it easier to bond with and talk to like-minded businesspeople in your industry. Then, after your surf, maybe you talk shop on the beach or in the parking lot . . . it makes for the perfect work-life balance."[18]

STOKE IS PRICELESS

It is said that everyone has his or her price. That adage was reportedly put to a $20 million dollar test when Hawaiian native and Heisman Trophy winning football quarterback Marcus Mariota entered into contract negotiations after being chosen in the first round draft of the National Football League. The Tennessee Titans offered him the high going-rate for prize players and drew up the standard contract. But for Mariota, there was a clause in the contract that clashed with his stoke: The Titans would not allow him to surf! Clauses like this are not uncommon in many sports. Contracts often exclude everything from motorcycling to skiing for fear of season or career-ending injury.

Surfline reported that Mariota supposedly balked at this.[19] Growing up in the surfing culture of Oahu, surfing and bodyboarding were part of him and the lessons learned in the water contributed to his success on the football field. Known for his calm and professional manner under game pressure, surfing had proven therapeutic and helped him get out of the spotlight, regroup, re-charge, and find peace of mind. Without the stoke of surfing he would be a different athlete, less prepared for the intense competition of professional sports. When all was said and done, Mariota worked out an agreement and signed his contract.

"Double his age, an entire generation of competitors had passed between us when I first met Kelly Slater on the North Shore in December of 1989," says Shaun Tomson in a *Surfer* magazine tribute.[20] "I was leaving the pro tour. Kelly was just 17. But as an analytical competitor, I considered it my job to evaluate anyone new coming up through the ranks." Tomson could tell immediately that Slater had incredible potential and "a future that was going to be written in bold letters . . . Kelly appeared on the scene with an aura of absolute confidence . . . unlike that of any young surfer I had ever seen. He had it all, and right then I could see he was going to take surfing down an entirely new road, and scarily, he saw it too."[21]

Fast-forward 25 years and Tomson's observations become prophetic. Slater holds and/or has shattered almost every record in competitive surfing. Yet his most significant contributions may have come from outside the competitions—the innovations he has made that have changed the sport of surfing itself. From his fresh approach to backside tube riding to his aerials, style, and moves *above* the wave, Slater has been able to *sustain and repeat* innovations along with winning an unprecedented number of championships.

It's interesting that when asked about his best surfing experience, Kelly does not mention any of his double-digit world titles, but rather, as he told Tomson "a nighttime session with buddy Shane Dorian at 'Restaurants' (Nomatu Island, Fiji)—pulling into phosphorescent barrels together on soft boards, lights strapped to their waists, watched by a group of shrieking Fijians."

Tomson's appreciation of Slater is testimony to how the models of excellence and the raising of the bar contributes to the ongoing stoke. "Kelly is at once the most popular surfer in the world and, after all these years, still its biggest enigma" he says. "But we need him. We need him to keep coming up with crazy designs, we need him to keep risking his life at Teahupo'o and Pipe, and we need him to keep breaking records, crushing competitors generations his junior. We need him to keep inspiring us."[22]

Slater's sheer dominance is a thing of beauty worth emulating. Tomson is so stoked by Slater's prowess and longevity that he says, "Quite simply, there is surfing before Kelly Slater, and then there is surfing now."[23] Before Slater: "BS". After Slater: "AS". But time does not stand still, and a young generation of Big Wave surfers is on the horizon to push the sport farther. Younger, "AS" surfers like Eddie Aikau Winner John John Florence, Billy Kemper, Nic Lamb, Maya Gabeira, Makua Rothman, Paige Alms, Albee Layer, Savannah Shaughnessy, Mason Ho and the ever-joyous Jamie O'Brien will surely raise the bar for men and women.

Every entrepreneur can learn a lot from Kelly Slater. Think of his many attributes as a checklist for innovators and entrepreneurs. He has *confidence* borne of his skill. He *prepares* hard and *studies the competition*. He *tests and retests* his moves until he perfects them. He has *style and flair* because he is equally as comfortable in his own skin as he is in the ocean. And he is *grateful for the opportunities* surfing has given him.

IT TAKES HOLD OF YOU

To hear Kelly Slater tell it, the stoke of surfing shaped him completely. "My life isn't at all normal, but it's my own creation from following what I really love. I'm sure I've missed out on a lot of things that are irreplaceable. I missed a lot of my daughter's childhood . . . I do miss those connections you get from just being near people you love all the time," he says. "But surfing has given me nearly everything. It's exposed me to so many great ideas and situations and challenges. It's provided me a life I couldn't have known otherwise. I've experienced such a deep and interconnected matrix of people around the world, and I never could have comprehended that just living in a small town in Florida."[24]

You can see from Kelly's remarks that in life you win some and lose some. He's traveled the world, but missed his daughter's early years. How many business men and business women have totally neglected their families to build a business? Life is full of choices and there are consequences for those choices. In business as in Big Wave surfing, it is a matter of priorities at any given point in time. The trick is to not try to "balance" life and work but to integrate them into each other.

Dale Webster is not a world champion or a household name in the surfing world, but in terms of stoke and longevity, his story is hard to beat. "September 3, 2015, marks 40 years in a row of me riding at least three waves to the beach, everyday. It started in 1975 during the swell known as 'The Monster from New Zealand,'" he says. "Each day that swell got bigger and more perfect, and the waves were so epic and so memorable that I told myself I had to keep practicing every day . . . I like to think of surfing as a healthy habit, but I understand how it can be an addiction. You're always checking the weather, the swell, and just getting amped about finding waves somewhere," he says. "And you do it all for those moments when the waves just seem to answer to whatever is on your mind. A really nice wave comes to you, you ride it, you kick out, and you hardly remember it because you were so in the now. That's the addictive part to me—that totally transcendent moment." Echoing Slater, Webster says his life "isn't at all normal, but it's my own creation from following what I really love . . . surfing has given me nearly everything."[25]

Herbie Fletcher of San Clemente, CA, is in the same stoke club as Kelly Slater and Dale Webster. "When I was 10 years old, I saw people surfing, and with my paper-route money I bought a wood surfboard for $27 and started surfing. I thought it was the greatest. When I was 16, Hobie [Hobart "Hobie" Alter] gave me a job filming with Bruce Brown, and we made a movie called *The Wet Set*," he recalls. "I made enough money to go to Hawaii to meet all the big-wave riders." Like many young entrepreneurs, he "did whatever it took to stay there. I'd sleep in the bushes; I'd sleep in Dewey Weber's car. All I had was a bedroll, a pair of trunks, and a surfboard. I gave up everything to go surfing. Surfing just took ahold of me. If you're a surfer, you go surfing. That's it. I'll never stop. Even when I can't paddle out anymore, I'll still be down at the beach staying up to date on what's happening and looking to the future of surfing."[26]

So, at the end of the day, "stoke" comes from inside us. And sustaining it often benefits from the company of others. Passion is passion. Exuberance is exuberance. Stoke is stoke, and ultimately, *staying* stoked is the name of the game in business, in surfing, and in life.

SURFER STEP
10

STAY STOKED

Passion is as vital in surfing as it is in business. It is an important source of energy and it's what keeps you going through the tough times. Big Wave surfers, as well as entrepreneurs, have the same fires burning. They go to sleep at night and awaken the next morning stoked for new opportunities. It is that fire, that desire, which keeps them fresh and makes the other nine lessons of The Surfer's Rules work.

Being an entrepreneur is not for everyone. The ups and downs, the risks, and the real-life challenges of successful entrepreneurs are well known: Are you prepared to take a second mortgage on your house to meet payroll? Would you sleep in your car to save money while on sales trips? Would you be willing to give part ownership in your company to grow and expand into new markets? These are difficult but necessary decisions.

"As with business, it's very often the people who don't follow the crowd that reap the rewards in surfing," says surfer and entrepreneur Ben Martin. "Those people who are prepared to take a chance and go a long way out of their way to search for new spots are the pioneers. Guaranteed, they're surfing perfect waves other people have never heard of right now. And when the bandwagon finds them, they'll find somewhere new. Always one step ahead of the game."[27]

What will carry the day for every entrepreneur and innovator is the deep belief in what they are doing, making, or selling. Stoke is as contagious in the world of business as it is in the lineup awaiting Big Waves.

Creativity and curiosity have to be your ally. Change has to be your partner. Taking smart risks is your new best friend.

To the innovators, entrepreneurs, and startups of the world, nothing fans the flames and stokes the fires more than a good idea taken to the marketplace successfully, followed by another . . . and another . . . and another. With Big Waves come Big Opportunities. Where there's a *will*, there's a WAVE. Stay stoked!

THINGS TO DO:

Now that you are an experienced and successful entrepreneur and innovator, it is time to share what you know and to give back. Here are three things you can do to share the stoke:

1. Find three young entrepreneurs and offer to mentor them.

2. Apply your skills to helping to solve one of the world's problems that is close to your heart. You pick the topic—e.g. the environment, war and peace, poverty, cancer research, education.

3. Support local organizations that are grooming the next generation.

EPILOGUE
MAKE YOUR OWN WAVES

THRIVING IN TODAY'S HIGHLY COMPETITIVE BUSINESS ENVI-
ronment requires departing from conventional thinking.
Doing the same thing in the same way and expecting better
results is a fool's journey. For many years, the world of business
has been represented metaphorically as behaving like a ma-
chine—but new times call for new thinking. Waves, sets, and
cycles offer a better biological model for today's entrepreneurs
and innovators.

In these pages I have taken the analogy linking business and
waves *literally*. Understanding how elite Big Wave surfers plan
and prepare for "waves" gives new insights into an entrepreneur
or innovator's "opportunity." The subject matter experts for
Make Your Own Waves are Big Wave surfers who challenge 30,
40, and 50-plus foot mountains of water. They understand

changing conditions, the power of preparation, and the physical and mental tools needed to produce results. They have to. It is a matter of life or death.

And surfing, as it turns out, has learned much from the world of business too—the sport is always undergoing tremendous changes. The future of Big Wave surfing looks bright and prosperous, with new developments already underway.

Atypical sponsors, like Target, Jeep, Pacifico, Tag Heuer and Samsung, are entering the arena. Traditionally sponsors have been "lifestyle"-related, like Quiksilver, RVCA, Oakley, Vans, Volcom, Hurley or O'Neill. In the future, expect sponsorships to come from companies that traditionally underwrite football, soccer, and baseball—think airlines, banks, and insurance companies.

More women are taking on Big Waves. The number of professional events, as well as gender parity in prize money for waterwomen, is on the rise—finally. Social media and Kickstarter are democratizing access for women. "Just 15 years ago, only 5 percent of surfers were women," says Super Sessions Founder Nico Sell. Super Sessions is a multimedia project that gives the world's most talented female Big Wave surfers the resources to record their most epic moments. The series follows 13 women around the globe as they video their own search for Big Waves. "What we're trying to do is something different," filmmaker and Big Wave surfer Grant Washburn said in the Super Sessions Kickstarter video. "In this kind of format, we think we have the ability to have everybody catch the best wave of their life." The women participating record themselves and then hold "digital roundtables" and review footage of their surfing in France, California, Ireland, South America, and Hawaii.[1] Kickstarter money goes directly to the women to underwrite the costs of their surf odysseys. The top five videos received prize money, as well.

Thanks to technology, more and more big surf spots are being discovered and the arrival of massive swells more carefully predicted. Add to this streaming live coverage of events, a smartphone or GoPro camera with footage posted on social media sites, and you have a recipe for the rapid growth of all-things related to surfing. New advances in wave-making machinery will bring surfing inland and offer its pleasures and challenges to millions more in the far, landlocked corners of the world.

And surfing will soon become an Olympic sport. This is a testimony to the rising participation and appreciation for the sport on a worldwide platform. As International Surfing Association president Fernando Aguerre says, "Surfing is truly a global sport, more popular and more widely practiced than many current Olympic sports. Surfing is pursued in every corner of the world, in more than a hundred countries. There are now over 35 million surfers worldwide!" "Surfers are a strong and positive influence on young people around the world. They are a very relevant part of our youth culture and serve as inspirational figures, naturally representing Olympic values."[2]

The parallels between surfing and entrepreneurship hold true as we look to the future of start-ups. Atypical funding sources like Kickstarter and Kiva.org are on the rise to subsidize innovation. More and more women are entering the start-up world with great success. Technology is opening new and unprecedented opportunities on a daily basis, worldwide. And though entrepreneurship will never be an Olympic sport, applying the rigor and preparation of elite athletes such as Big Wave surfers will pave a path to the podium.

Though the number of entrepreneurs who are surfers is growing, The Surfer's Rules offered here do not require that you be a skilled surfer in order to be a successful entrepreneur.

Land-locked innovation "hubs" are rising up in places as far apart as Berlin, Germany; Northwest Arkansas; and Kerala, India. Wisdom knows no geographical boundaries.

The Surfer's Rules offer 10 lessons in *unconventional wisdom* that will serve as a guide to anyone seeking to be a successful entrepreneur or innovator. Rocket science is not required. Venture capital funds are not mandatory. And a special "genius gene" in your DNA is not necessary.

What is required is the planning, preparation, patience, and passion that is at the core of every Big Wave surfer . . . and every entrepreneur. A mindset, skillset, and toolset that follows the model of The Surfer's Rules will surely help guide you on your journey. Fortunately, everything you need is conveniently located inside your head . . . and your heart. From learning to swim to staying stoked, it's time to make your own waves.

AFTERWORD

by Cathy Rodgers

FOR THOSE OF US WHO HAVE FOUND OUR "INNER MAVERICK," there is the unquenchable desire to do the extraordinary. We share uncompromised belief that bold moves will differentiate us. Our restlessness grows to counter the mundane, and we have a palatable discontent with the boredom that invariably increases as things get more predictable. For passionate visionaries there is a clock that ticks loudly in our head and heart– reminding us constantly that life is short and meant to be lived to the fullest, on the edge, with an unwavering belief we can push the limits and that boundaries are meant to be redefined.

For the entrepreneur, like the big wave surfer, there is an undisputed internal acknowledgement that preparation is essential, sacrifice a given, laser-like focus on the goal mandatory. It requires research, study, and the development of a clear strategy, the visualization of a goal, and the execution of a game plan with surgical precision. It is this combination of uncompromised passion and tenacious dedication that elevates one's game. It's a self-confidence that resonates like an aura, but with a pragmatic understanding of the risk. Like Big Wave surfers, elite performers recognize that being in the right place at the right time is still a dependent variable. Unwavering willpower, tenacity of spirit, sustained optimism, and ultra-resiliency are prerequisites. As the elite know, one must be incessantly "ready" for the moment, when it finally presents itself. It is an "all in" investment requiring an inner fearlessness and the realization—in spite of all the preparation—one can still lose it all.

It is this "go big" or "go home", high-risk/high-reward philosophy. It is a blatant disdain for the status quo, preferring to live life fully, to dare to dream, to dare to do. It is unquenchable enthusiasm, eternal optimism, and an undeterred belief that one can change the world. Big Wave surfers and today's entrepreneurs all seem to share this quest to "unleash" one's true and ultimate potential, knowing full well the odds against them and the possible consequences: a triple wave hold down, a business under water.

Those who emerge as successful entrepreneurs are those individuals who become, in and of themselves, forces of nature. Their achievements are realized not with reckless abandon, but in a decidedly clear and compelling manner. They have an unfiltered vision of the possible, an uncompromised level of preparation. They hone necessary skills, have a complete trust in their judgement and instinct, and have a belief in their ability to navigate even in uncharted turbulent waters. It is commitment and tenacity matched by an unwavering fearlessness. It is a courage built on confidence, coupled with a raw ability that allows the visionary to leave the lineup, drop in, and, if all goes to plan, unleash a performance with an outcome few have ever imagined. It is this singular moment, this culmination of preparation and confidence that redefines us and our world.

This is the world of innovators and entrepreneurs, where the rule book is "ripped" up, where conventional wisdom is replaced by curiosity. It is a world where the desire to succeed is built on a willingness to fail, where comfort is unnerving, and stress is the edge that sharpens focus. These are the qualities that capture our imagination, the leadership traits that ignite a level of excitement and awe in us all. It is the mastery of skills that redefine the art of the possible. Spectators become believers. Experience becomes accessible. Paradigms are forever altered, new rules emerge for new targets to break, new markets to crack, and new brands to create.

Big waves and big ideas happen anywhere in the world, but there are things we can do to improve the odds of success and create the optimum conditions of opportunity. Extreme wave riders monitor and await the right wind and weather conditions that produce the right swells in a handful of infamous big wave locations around the world. Similarly, today's most savvy entrepreneurs are migrating to the hot beds of innovation and immersing themselves in the culture of creation. It is to these innovation destinations where the top talent has gravitated, the angel investors hover, and ideas flourish in a petri dish of experimentation. These are places where like minds push each other to stretch the limits of their own preconceived notions and the propensity for productive output is more a question of when, not if.

So it is with this tolerance for ambiguity, this comfort with the unpredictable, that the enlightened entrepreneurs and the visionary Big Wave surfers converge at those places that mesmerize and amaze. Wherever the talent "line up" is extraordinary there is the inner recognition that if you can distinguish yourself here, you are among the best of the best. From Silicon Valley to Shipstearns Bluff, Tel Aviv to Todos Santos, Boston to Bonzai, Seattle to Nazaré, Toronto to Teahupo'o, and London to Dungeons; the risk and the reward draw those who want to shape the future, those who dare to dream of a destiny and a legacy.

While many entrepreneurs may aspire to create that next breakthrough product, to be the next unicorn, it is important to note innovation and "daring big" are not limited to the blank canvas of the emerging company. In fact, according to Boston Consulting Group's 2015 perspectives on the most consistently innovative companies over the past decade, four of the companies, Toyota, BMW, IBM, and GE are more than 100 years old, joined by Apple, HP, Nike, and Microsoft, all boasting over four decades of research and innovation.

These companies have much in common: a culture of innovation; a commitment to invest in research; a recognition that technology can and must be leveraged to enable change; and knowledge that the next great thing will not be realized if one stays within their swim lane.

Speaking from my experience within IBM, our success has been dependent on the spirit and determination of the intrapreneur. It is our wild ducks, our equivalent to the Big Wave surfers of the corporate world, who consciously choose to fly out of formation, who have contributed to our long history of restlessly reinventing ourselves. It's this cultural DNA, this pulsating current of creativity that has positioned IBM as a consistent catalyst for change over the years.

No company survives that chooses to rest on its laurels. It takes fearlessness to challenge the status quo and define the next aha moment. It takes grit to resist falling into the trap of "sameness." It means that being agile is more than just an action verb. A company thrives when it commits to leading without compromise and when its employees know they too can lead without needing permission.

So whether it is the Big Wave purists who paddle in on long boards, or those who favor leveraging technology and new techniques that allow a tow-in to the massive monsters yet to be conquered, or whether it is leash line, foot holds, or the next generation of foil boarders . . . we do not yet know where the limits are. We see maverick startups every day in the business world: Uber, Xiami, Airbnb, Snapchat, Pinterest. And we've seen the big waves coming in from Google, Amazon, Apple, and Tesla. It's hard not to want in on some of that genuine, authentic big business wave action, knowing it's the real deal.

As we have learned from Big Wave sufers, at their core is a way of thinking, a way of acting, a way of pushing the limits. It's a preference for getting out of the comfort zone, off the beach, and into the water.

Waves are incessant, and so too there is no limit to the human imagination. For every boundary now defined, there are those thinking, dreaming, and daring to challenge and change it.

If all this were easy, everyone would do it. That said, after reading *Make Your Own Waves*, it is very clear that anyone can try. Now drop in and shred!

ACKNOWLEDGMENTS

MAKE YOUR OWN WAVES WOULD LITERALLY NOT HAVE BEEN written were it not for the vision of the senior editor at AMACOM Books, Stephen S. Power. About a year ago, via my trusted literary agent John Willig, I submitted an ambitious proposal for a book on innovation that would have chronicled my 20 years of research on skills and tools of successful innovators and entrepreneurs. In the book proposal a small section was to be devoted to "The Surfer's Rules" as an illustration of one of my findings: innovators often take analogies and metaphors literally. Stephen contacted John and said, in effect, "that's a pretty interesting book idea, but what *really* interests me is the section about the surfers. I think that would be a very good read for any entrepreneur." Stephen and I had a phone conversation, I gave it some thought, and I put together a new proposal. Within a day of submitting the proposal a contract was under way.

One of The Surfer's Rules is "Never Surf Alone." It certainly holds true here. My wife, Catherine, my five children Kale, Elina, Caitlin, Johana and Kellin and even the young grandkids Sienna, Celesse, Mila, Mari and Kai were all enthusiastic and supportive, each in their own way.

At my company, www.TheBITGroup.com, Richelle Fortin, was invaluable to the research, analysis and project management needed from start to finish. Sheryl Posner and Miranda Pennington did a wonderful job of editing and fact checking outside their normal range. And my dear friend, advertising design legend Mike Moser, who recently passed away, was a constant source of fresh ideas and encouragement.

Truth be told, I am a much more accomplished baseball player than surfer, having won four amateur baseball World Series rings in the last ten years. But I love the ocean and I first wrote a few pages about The Surfer's Rules in 1991 in the *New York Times* bestseller, *If It Ain't Broke. . .BREAK IT!* I've been around the surfing community most of my life, having grown up in Southern California and then living for a dozen years in the beach town of Bolinas, CA and spending close to 20 summers in Hanalei, Kauai. I have also spent several years on the world's oceans aboard university ships circling the globe, teaching on Colorado State University's wonderful Semester at Sea program.

But it was in Hanalei that my first exposure to Big Wave surfers happened. A few years later came visits to Maverick's, near my home in Northern California, to watch and talk with an elite group of impressive men and women who ride waves the size of office buildings. That said, I knew that I was far from being an expert on Big Wave surfing or surfing history, so I am grateful for the close reading of the manuscript by surf historian Patrick Moser, and for the meticulous, no-nonsense feedback from World Champion surfer Shaun Tomson.

"As you have seen, each chapter began with an opening section, largely devoted to the mindset, skillset and toolset of Big Wave surfers. This is followed by a series of "Steps" that summarized how a given Rule related to business. Chapters closed with "Things to Do" which business readers often revisit and apply it to their own projects or ideas. This section of each chapter drew upon my long experience with training programs. My latest, *Innovating for Results TM*, includes core elements from The Surfer's Rules. My thanks to everyone at ORConsulting and High Performance Learning for feedback on my *Innovating for Results(TM)* program.

IBM's Cathy Rodgers' *Afterword* reminded me that entrepreneurs can also come from within large companies, and BAE Systems CEO Linda Hudson showed me what happens when this is encouraged. Shaun Tomson reiterated how much courage it takes to fully commit to surfing huge waves... and to your business's big dreams. I am in debt to them both. Several Big Wave surfers were generous with their time and wisdom, especially Nic Lamb, Maya Gabeira and Jeff Clark whose comments and insights made me re-visit and revise some of the Surfer's Rules. A shout out also goes to Tavarua boat captain and GoPro manager Steven Baker for his guidance and perspective.

Lastly, there are many others to thank for their wisdom and encouragement along the way. Amy Robinson, Paul Tomita, Dorothy Van Hoorn, and Jeff Amerine were especially helpful in keeping me in the world of the entrepreneur when the Big Wave surfing world kept seducing me. Speaker agents Jon and Marc Reede of Rave Speakers gave wise counsel and feedback. Dozens of colleagues were kind enough to peruse the manuscript, offer feedback and write endorsements, and to them I am most grateful: Jim Kouzes, Anthony Vidergauz, Jim Patrick, Fasie Malherbe, Sheila Heen, Steve Cohen, Peter Pattenden, Parker Lee, Holly Stiel, John Suttle, Les McCabe, Michael Bennett, Paul Tomita, Al Calarco, Marilou McFarlane, Bernie Nagle, Marion McGovern, Kristin Luna, and George Kam.

I learned so much in writing this book that I find myself using ideas from it on a daily basis. I hope readers will feel the same way. And I'm more stoked than ever!

NOTES

PROLOGUE

1   Robert Kriegel and Louis Patler, *If It Ain't Broke . . . BREAK IT!: Unconventional Wisdom for a Changing Business World.* (New York: Time Warner Books, 1991).

2   "Fitness Icon Gabby Reece Spills on Sex and Her Private Life with Surfing Star Laird Hamilton," Gabrielle Reese, POPSUGAR video, 4:05, June 26, 2013, www.popsugar .com/celebrity/Gabby-Reece-Interview-Her-New-Book-Video-30878219.

3   Shaun Tomson interview, August 13, 2015. Santa Barbara, CA.

4   Steven Baker phone interview, June 3, 2015.

CHAPTER 1: LEARN TO SWIM

1   Jordy Smith, "Advice to the Class of 2015," *Surfer,* March 23, 2015, www.surfermag .com/features/jordy-smith-advice-to-the-hot-100/#G0LrEAwwpm4chTec.97.

2   Juliann Johnson, "5 of Surfing's Most Successful Entrepreneurs," *The Inertia,* September 10, 2013, www.theinertia.com/surf/5-most-successful-surfing-entrepreneurs/.

3   Matt Warshaw, *Maverick's: The Story of Big-Wave Surfing* (San Francisco: Chronicle Books, 2000).

4   Ibid., 45.

CHAPTER 2: GET WET

1   "A Morning With . . . Julian Wilson," *Swell,* www.swell.com/!LmjTzTalRX3sm813 -f-2tA!/10-pieces-of-must-read-surf-advice-from-julian-wilson.

2   *The Mark Healey Blog,* "About Mark Healey," accessed January 2016, markhealeywaterman .com/about/.

3   "Nazaré—Big Sunday: As Big as It Gets," YouTube video, posted by Pedro Miranda, February 6, 2014, www.youtube.com/watch?v=awjMSjic268.

4   "Talk Story: Garrett McNamara," *Surfline* video, www.surfline.com/surflinetv /featured-clips/talk-story-garrett-mcnamara_126900.

5   "How Big Companies Can Innovate," McKinsey & Company, February 2015, www .mckinsey.com/insights/innovation/how_big_companies_can_innovate?cid=other -eml-alt-mip-mck-oth-1502.

6   Shaun Tomson and Patrick Moser, *Surfer's Code* (Salt Lake City: Gibbs Smith, 2006).

7   "On Etiquette," Rob Gilley, *Surfer* Magazine, April 27, 2015, www.surfermag.com /features/surf-etiquette/#jfYydD0qHkAwxSEz.99.

8   Ibid.

9   Ashtyn Douglas, "Surfers Are Assholes," *Surfer* Magazine, May 21, 2015, www
     .surfermag.com/features/surfers-are-assholes/#W7VidoqzBqkzd3YZ.99.

10   Ibid.

11   Ibid.

12   Liz Wiseman, *Rookie Smarts* (New York: Harper Business, 2014).

13   Kristin Sainani, "What, Me Worry?," *Stanford* magazine, May 2, 2014.

14   Ibid.

15   Grant Baker, *Surfer* Magazine, www.surfermag.com/features/talking-mavs-with-twiggy
     -baker-the-finest-line/#oiEZY6h1cqqfg1rx.97

16   Timothy Leary, www.surfsplendorpodcast.com/2014/04/

17   Anne Lamott's Facebook page, April 8, 2015,www.facebook.com/AnneLamott
     /posts/662177577245222.

18   "How Should You Tap Into Silicon Valley?" McKinsey & Company, September 2015, www
     .mckinsey.com/insights/business_technology/how_should_you_tap_into_silicon
     _valley?cid=digital-eml-alt-mkq-mck-oth-1509.

19   Catherine E. Toth, "Entrepreneurs Inspired by the Ocean," *Hawaii Business*, February 2014,
     www.hawaiibusiness.com/entrepreneurs-inspired-by-the-ocean/.

CHAPTER 3: DECIDE TO RIDE

1   Shaun Tomson interview, August 13, 2015. Santa Barbara, CA.

2   Reef McIntosh, YouTube video, www.youtube.com/watch?v=szdsYSgKwcA&index=1
     &list=PLpi1EAR1PAPd4dMnnRQ69Dm8S9nPuLRXr

3   "The Leadership Power That Comes from Inexperience," First Round Review, *Fast Company*,
     February 9, 2015, www.fastcompany.com/3042024/hit-the-ground-running/the-leader
     ship-power-that-comes-from-inexperience.

4   Lorraine Twohill, "How Google Breaks Through," *McKinsey Quarterly*, February 2015.

5   "Mavericks Legend—Darryl Flea Virostko," YouTube video, posted by FleaHab, June 29,
     2012, https://www.youtube.com/watch?v=-Rv1oOX5Gmc.

6   Louis Patler, *Don't Compete, TILT the Field!* (Oxford, UK: Capstone/John Wiley & Co.: 1999).

7   Lia Huber, "Anything Is Possible," *Parade*, March 1, 2015, www.parade.com/378875
     /parade/anything-is-possible/.

8   "74 inspirational Quotes That Will Change Your Life," MSN.com, February 8, 2015, www
     .msn.com/en-us/lifestyle/mind-and-soul/74-inspirational-quotes-that-will-change-your-life
     /ss-AA9arib#image=74.

9   Nicholas Mohnacky, "What Surfing Can Teach You About Entrepreneurship," *Entrepreneur*,
     October 30, 2014, www.entrepreneur.com/article/239130.

10   John Gustafson, "Blood in the Surf: How Big-Wave Surfer Greg Long Made Peace with the
     Ocean," *The Guardian*, March 23, 2015, www.theguardian.com/sport/2015/mar/23/blood-in
     -the-surf-how-big-wave-surfer-greg-long-made-peace-with-the-ocean.

11   "Big Wave Surfers," *Club of the Waves*, accessed January 2016, www.clubofthewaves.com
     /surf-culture/big-wave-surfers.php.

12   Laird Hamilton, "Big Wave Surfing—Laird Hamilton," *Surfing Zones*, August 19, 2015,
     www.surfingzones.com/big-wave-surfing-famous.

13   Garrett James, "Kelly Slater Is His Own Biggest Critic," *Surfer* Magazine, April 7, 2015,
     www.surfermag.com/blogs/random-happenings/kelly-slater-biggest-critic/#jOG
     tEOcIthFK35yG.99.

NOTES

14   John Gustafson, "Blood in the Surf: How Big-Wave Surfer Greg Long Made Peace with the Ocean," *The Guardian*, March 23, 2015, www.theguardian.com/sport/2015/mar/23 /blood-in-the-surf-how-big-wave-surfer-greg-long-made-peace-with-the-ocean.

15   Andy Irons, "#25 Dane Reynolds," *Surfer* Magazine, July 22, 2010, www.surfermag.com /features/number_25_dane_reynolds/#28HwRIcAj0f3Ztau.97

16   Laird Hamilton, "Big Wave Surfing—Laird Hamilton," *Surfing Zones*, August 19, 2015, www.surfingzones.com/big-wave-surfing-famous.

17   Shawn Dollar, *Mav News*, www./mavsurfer.com/frank_quirarte_photo/?page_id=23.

18   Nic Lamb interview, August 20, 2015, Santa Monica, CA.

19   Abishek Khan, "Auroville's Surfer Girl and Entrepreneur," September 29, 2014, www.redbull .com/in/en/surfing/stories/1331681677512/auroville-s-surfer-girl-and-entrepreneur.

CHAPTER 4: ALWAYS LOOK "OUTSIDE"

1   Andrew Cave, "Twitter Cofounder Biz Stone's Seven Secrets For Starting And Leading A Successful Business," *Forbes*, June 18, 2014, www.forbes.com/sites/andrewcave/2014/06/18 /twitter-co-founder-biz-stones-seven-secrets-for-starting-and-leading-a-successful-business/

2   "*Surfline's* Big Wave Roundtable 2012—Uncut," YouTube video, posted by *Surfline*, September 15, 2014, www.youtube.com/watch?v=RCunB1DG9as.

3   Ibid., 17:50.

4   Shaun Tomson interview, August 13, 2015, Santa Barbara, CA.

5   David and Anatole Lokshin qtd in Crishana Haynes, "GPS device Trace partners with Oakley Lowers Pro," GrindTV.com, April 30, 2015, www.grindtv.com/surf/gps-device -trace-partners-oakley-lowers-pro/#eoO14melb3KhVlrQ.97

6   Timothy Leary, surfsplendorpodcast.com/2014/04/

7   John Sculley, "Do you want to sell sugared water . . .," Youtube video, www.youtube .com/watch?v=S_JYy_0XUe8.

8   Johnny Ive, *The New Yorker*, Feb. 23, 2015, www.newyorker.com/magazine/2015/02/23 /shape-things-come?utm_content=bufferb120e&utm_medium=social&utm_source =facebook.com&utm_campaign=buffer

9   Johnny Ive, *The New Yorker*, Feb. 23, 2015, www.newyorker.com/magazine/2015/02/23 /shape-things-come?

10   Ian Parker, "The Shape of Things to Come," *The New Yorker*, Feb. 23, 2015.

11   Ibid.

12   "Top Surfers Name the World's Most Dangerous Waves, Plus Surf Spots for the Rest of Us," *National Geographic*, July 3, 2013, www.adventureblog.nationalgeographic.com/2013/07/03 /the-worlds-8-most-dangerous-waves-plus-surf-spots-for-the-rest-of-us/.

13   Ibid.

14   Ibid.

15   Ibid.

16   Pete Thomas, "Pro surfer Mark Healey 'Obliterated' in Massive Puerto Escondido Barrel," GrindTV video, May 4, 2015, www.grindtv.com/surf/pro-surfer-mark-healey -obliterated-in-massive-puerto-escondido-barrel/#ChUT27EbHgrRuU4F.99.

17   "Welcome," accessed January 2016, www.pacificsurfpartners.com.

18   Freddy Patacchai, "Freddy P's North Shore Survival Tips," March 12, 2015, www .quiksilver.com/blog/surf/20141021232453NEWS287059004833.html.

19   Ibid.

20   Nic Lamb interview, August 20, 2015, Santa Monica, CA.

21   David Butler and Linda Tischler, "The Startup Revolution Is About to Surge Again," *Fast Company*, February 2015.

22   Jeff Clark interview, August 12, 2015, Pillar Point, CA.

23   Matt Warshaw, "Why I Love Barton Lynch," *Surfer*, August 25, 2015, www .surfermag.com/blogs/eos/why-i-love-barton-lynch/#FEMVRU8eFLVqcDc1.99.

24   "Ken Romanzi, '82," accessed January 2016, www.action.babson.edu/#ken.

CHAPTER 5: COMMIT, CHARGE, SHRED!

1   "Happy Birthday, Andy Irons," *Surfing* Magazine, July 23, 2015, www.surfing magazine.com/video/happy-birthday-andy-irons/.

2   Ibid.

3   Pete Thomas, "Pro Surfer Mark Healey 'Obliterated' in Massive Puerto Escondido Barrel," GrindTV video, May 4, 2015, www.grindtv.com/surf/pro-surfer-mark-healey -obliterated-in-massive-puerto-escondido-barrel/#ChUT27EbHgrRuU4F.99

4   Nicholas Mohnacky, "What Surfing Can Teach You About Entrepreneurship," *Entrepreneur*, October 30, 2014, www.entrepreneur.com/article/239130.

5   Ibid.

6   Justin Housman, "Big Wave Bianca," *Surfer*, February 5, 2015, www .surfermag.com/features/bianca-valenti/#VF32HrIlihpHvxMq.99

7   "Greg Long: Big Wave Rider," YouTube video, posted by *National Geographic*, November 24, 2014, www.youtube.com/watch?v=iPxfCYlWVWw.

8   Shaun Tomson interview, August 13, 2015, Santa Barbara, CA.

9   Timothy Leary, www.surfsplendorpodcast.com/2014/04/

10   Barry Punzal, "Gerhardt balances life as mother, professor, scientist, big-wave surfer," *Presidio Sports*, February 6, 2011, www.presidiosports.com/2011/02/gerhardt -balances-life-as-mother-professor-scientist-big-wave-surfer/.

11   "Greg Long: Big Wave Rider," YouTube video, posted by *National Geographic*, November 24, 2014, www.youtube.com/watch?v=iPxfCYlWVWw.

12   Shaun Tomson and Patrick Moser, *Surfer's Code* (Salt Lake City: Gibbs Smith, 2006).

13   Shaun Tomson, www.shauntomson.com.

14   Matt Bromley, *Surfing* Magazine, www.surfingmagazine.com/photos/the-biggest-wave-ever -paddled-into-in-indo/.

15   Ryan Seelbach, "This and Nothing Else," www.redbull.tv/episodes/AP-1GVC3E73S2111/ ryan-seelbach.

16   "This and Nothing Else: Alex Martins," *Surfing* Magazine, February 23, 2015, www.surfing magazine.com/video/alex-martins-mavericks-735/.

17   Matt Skenazy, "Maya Gabiera Takes a Breath," *Outside*, September 3, 2014. www .outsideonline.com/1925936/maya-gabeira-takes-breath.

18   Ibid.

19   Ibid.

20   Ibid.

21   Ibid.

22   Matt Warshaw, *Maverick's: The Story of Big-Wave Surfing* (San Francisco: Chronicle Books, 2000), 91.

NOTES

23   Ryan Seelbach, "This and Nothing Else," www.redbull.tv/episodes/AP-1GVC3E7
      3S2111/ryan-seelbach.

24   "Happy Birthday, Andy Irons," *Surfing* Magazine, July 23, 2015, www.surfingmag
      azine.com/video/happy-birthday-andy-irons/.

25   "Chasing the Swell," YouTube video, posted by Sachi Cunningham, October 14, 2012, www.
      youtube.com/watch?v=bkprsIaoIv0.

26   26 Timothy Leary, www.surfsplendorpodcast.com/2014/04/

27   "Oakley Wave of the Winter Documentary," YouTube video, posted by *Surfline*,
      November 25, 2014, www.youtube.com/watch?v=szdsYSgKwcA&index=1&
      list=PLpi1EAR1PAPd4dMnnRQ69Dm8S9nPuLRXr.

28   "All the Wood Behind One Arrow," www.findery.com/johnfox/notes/all-the-wood
      -behind-one-arrow.

CHAPTER 6: PADDLE BACK OUT

1   Patrick Moser, *Pacific Passages: An Anthology of Surf Writing* (Honolulu: University of Hawai'i
      Press, 2008), 138.

2   Ibid., 141.

3   Ibid., 138–139.

4   Ibid., 139.

5   Ibid., 141–142.

6   Ibid., 142.

7   "The Best Big Wave Surfers of All Time," *Surfer Today*, www.surfertoday.com
      /surfing/7446-the-best-big-wave-surfers-of-all-time.

8   Neil Patel, "90% of startups Fail: Here's What You Need to Know About the 10%," *Forbes*,
      January 16, 2015, www.forbes.com/sites/neilpatel/2015/01/16/90-of
      -startups-will-fail-heres-what-you-need-to-know-about-the-10/.

9   Lia Huber, "Anything is Possible," *Parade*, February 27, 2015, www.parade
      .com/378875/parade/anything-is-possible/.

10   Ben Martin, "Why Surfers Make Great Entrepreneurs (And Vice Versa)," March 21, 2014.
      www.blog.up.co/2014/03/21/surfers-make-great-entrepreneurs-vice-versa/.

11   Jordy Lawler, "Paying to Play," *Surfer*, April 15, 2015, www.surfermag.com/videos
      /jordy-lawler-paying-to-play/#fAvSdZgFfBMHCwMd.99.

12   "The Best Big Wave Surfers of All Time," *Surfer Today*, www.surfertoday.com
      /surfing/7446-the-best-big-wave-surfers-of-all-time.

13   Jordy Lawler, "Paying to Play," *Surfer*, April 15, 2015, www.surfermag.com/videos
      /jordy-lawler-paying-to-play/#fAvSdZgFfBMHCwMd.99.

14   Bruce Jenkins, "Big Waves Lure Surfers to Maverick's Competition," *San Francisco Chronicle*,
      January 24, 2014, www.sfgate.com/sports/jenkins/article/Big-waves-lure-surfers-to
      -Mavericks-competition-5169941.php.

15   Ibid.

16   John Gustafson, "Blood in the Surf: How Big-Wave Surfer Greg Long Made Peace wth the
      Ocean," *The Guardian*, March 23, 2015, www.theguardian.com/sport/2015/mar/23
      /blood-in-the-surf-how-big-wave-surfer-greg-long-made-peace-with-the-ocean.

17   Jordy Lawler, "Paying to Play," *Surfer*, April 15, 2015, www.surfermag.com/videos
      /jordy-lawler-paying-to-play/#fAvSdZgFfBMHCwMd.99.

18   Justin Housman, "Talking Mav's With Twiggy Baker," *Surfer*, May 5, 2015, www

.surfermag.com/features/talking-mavs-with-twiggy-baker-the-finest-line/#4rT 2R5QyuTZ36k2c.99.

19 Garrett James, "The Wipeout of the Year," *Surfer*, May 8, 2015, www.surfermag.com /features/the-wipeout-of-the-year-pedro-calado/#SKDvBxcAutCQdJoT.97.

20 "Life Lessons from Big-Wave Surfer Mark Matthews," *GrindTV* video, May 28, 2015, www .grindtv.com/surf/life-lessons-from-big-wave-surfer-mark-mathews/?sm_id=social _aumogrindtvhub_GrindTV_20150528_46592276&adbid=10152967402099895&ad bpl=fb&adbpr=8782279894#bGjTATxjCyp85Ro4.97.

21 Nic Lamb interview, August 20, 2015, Santa Monica, CA.

22 Paige Alms. www.surfgirlmag.com/2015/10/21/paige-alms-the-wave-i-ride/#.VtNsU2QrInU.

23 Keala Kennelly. www.worldsurfleague.com/posts/106193/kennelly-wins-surf-n-sea-pipeline -womens-pro

24 Matt Skenazy, "Maya Gabiera Takes a Breath," *Outside*, September 3, 2014. www .outsideonline.com/1925936/maya-gabeira-takes-breath.

25 "Talk Story: Garrett McNamara," Surfline video, www.surfline.com/surflinetv /featured-clips/talk-story-garrett-mcnamara_126900.

26 Matt Skenazy, "Maya Gabiera Takes a Breath," *Outside*, September 3, 2014. www .outsideonline.com/1925936/maya-gabeira-takes-breath.

27 Shaun Tomson interview, August 13, 2015, Santa Barbara.

28 Mark "Doc" Renneker. www.fearproject.net/the-doctors-diagnoses-on-fear/

29 Todd Prodanovich, *Surfer*, July 6, 2015, www.surfermag.com/features /big-wave-boot-camp/#uueuTjZT1V0gjzZ3.97.

30 Matt Bromley. www.surfingmagazine.com/photos/the-biggest-wave-ever-paddled -into-in-indo/

31 "10 Surfing Life Lessons from Jack Viorel," GrindTV video, May 14, 2015, www .grindtv.com/surf/10-surfing-life-lessons-from-jack-viorel/#dz8j4PJMweJ7uxjZ.97.

32 Jeff Clark interview, August 12, 2015, Pillar Point, CA.

33 Nic Lamb interview, August 20, 2015, Santa Monica, CA.

34 Bradshaw, Ken, "Interview: Ken Bradshaw, Wave Warrior," PBS.org, June 15, 2008, www.pbs. org/wnet/nature/condition-black-interview-ken-bradshaw-wave-warrior/1868/

35 Vikas Shaw, "Master of Invention," *Business Life*, September 2015, p. 24.

36 Steve Jobs, "Commencement Speech," (Stanford University, Stanford, CA, June 12, 2005). news.stanford.edu/news/2005/june15/jobs-061505.html

CHAPTER 7: NEVER TURN YOUR BACK ON THE OCEAN

1 Stuart Holmes Coleman, Eddie Would Go: The Story of Eddie Aikau, Hawaiian Hero and Pioneer of Big Wave Surfing. (New York: St. Martin's Press, 2001), 75.

2 Ibid.

3 Ibid.

4 Maya Gabeira interview, July 10, 2015.

5 "I'm Keala Kennelly and I'm a Surfer: Keala Kennelly at TEDxMalibu," YouTube video, posted by TEDx Talks, February 2, 2014, https://www.youtube.com/watch?v=eSvsr zPCZ5o.

6 Jai Bednall, "Keala Kennelly Rides 'One of the Heaviest Waves' Kelly Slater Has Ever Seen," July 24, 2015, www.news.com.au/sport/sports-life/keala-kennelly-rides-one -of-the-heaviest-waves-kelly-slater-has-ever-seen/story-fno61i58-1227455161468.

NOTES

7   Ibid.

8   Ibid.

9   Ibid.

10   Ibid.

11   "Shark Attacks Mick Fanning at J-Bay Open," YouTube video, posted by World Surf League, July 19, 2015, www.youtube.com/watch?v=xrt27dZ7DOA.

12   "Mick Fanning on 60 Minutes," posted by *Surfer*, August 3, 2015, www.surfermag .com/videos/mick-fanning-on-60-minutes/#zR6IAWSoJdSWBc7Q.97.

13   Ibid.

14   Ibid.

15   "Bethany Hamilton: Shark Attack—The Real Story," YouTube video, posted by Ayanna Murray, January 11, 2010, www.youtube.com/watch?v=ZnyopNkTWsU.

16   Ibid.

17   "Bethany Hamilton: Shark Attack—The Real Story," YouTube video, posted by Ayanna Murray, January 11, 2010, www.youtube.com/watch?v=ZnyopNkTWsU

18   Jeff Clark interview, August 12, 2015, Pillar Point, CA.

19   "This and Nothing Else: Alex Martins," *Surfing* Magazine, February 23, 2015, www .surfingmagazine.com/video/alex-martins-mavericks-735/.

20   "Ocean Waves," Monterrey Institute, www.montereyinstitute.org/noaa/lesson09 /l9text.htm.

21   Shaun Tomson interview, Santa Barbara, CA, August 13, 2015.

22   Ben Martin, "Why Surfers Make Great Entrepreneurs (And Vice Versa)," March 21, 2014. blog.up.co/2014/03/21/surfers-make-great-entrepreneurs-vice-versa/.

23   Kevin Starr, "Getting Beyond Hype: Four Questions to Predict Real Impact," *Stanford Social Innovation Review*, September 2, 2014.

CHAPTER 8: DARE BIG

1   John Hagel and John Seely Brown, "Innovating on the Edge of Big Waves," Bloomberg Business, January 30, 2008, www.bloomberg.com/bw/stories/2008-01-30/innovating-on-the -edge-of-big-wavesbusinessweek-business-news-stock-market-and-financial-advice.

2   Ibid.

3   "A Lifetime of Experience Leads to New Life-Safety Vest," September 6, 2013, www .jeffclarkMaverick's.com/news/2013/09/06/life-safety-vest/.

4   Ibid.

5   Ibid.

6   Ibid.

7   Ibid.

8   Ibid.

9   Ibid.

10   "Riding the Waves of Innovation–Surfing the Engine of Economic Growth–Catch the Wave, or Risk Wipe-Out . . . ," *BizShifts*, June 17, 2015, www.bizshifts-trends .com/2015/06/17/riding-the-waves-of-innovation-surfing-the-engine-of-economic -growth-catch-the-wave-or-risk-wipe-out/.

11   Ibid.

12 "74 inspirational Quotes That Will Change Your Life," MSN.com February 8, 2015, www
    .msn.com/en-us/lifestyle/mind-and-soul/74-inspirational-quotes-that-will-change-your-life
    /ss-AA9arib#image=74.

13 Ian Parker, "The Shape of Things to Come," *The New Yorker*, Feb. 23, 2015.

14 "Unconventional Wisdom: Shaun Tomson," *Surfer*, June 24. 2015, www.surfermag
    .com/features/unconventional-wisdom-shaun-tomson/#73fSRzo58h1eA27D.99.

15 Ibid.

16 Ibid.

17 Nico Guilis, "Secrets of the Ultimate Surfer Girl," *Harper's Bazaar*, April 7, 2015, www
    .harpersbazaar.com/culture/features/a10504/secrets-of-the-ultimate-surfer-girl/.

18 Will Connors, "Maya Gabeira is Back Riding the Big Wave," *The Wall Street Journal*, March
    10. 2015, www.wsj.com/articles/maya-gabeira-is-back-riding-the-big-wave-1426014299.

19 "I'm Keala Kennelly and I'm a Surfer: Keala Kennelly at TEDxMalibu," YouTube video,
    posted by TEDx Talks, February 2, 2014, https://www.youtube.com/watch?v=eSvsrzPCZ5o.

20 "Kevin Weil, SVP of Product, Twitter," *Fast Company*, www.fastcompany.com/3043920
    /most-creative-people-2015/kevin-weil.

21 Jeff Mull, "According to Pancho." *Surfer*, August 27, 2015, www.surfermag.com
    /features/according-to-pancho/#V57xE1mIyvtbY4I0.99.

22 Bruce Jenkins, "Big Waves Lure Surfers to Maverick's Competition," *San Francisco Chronicle*,
    January 24, 2014, www.sfgate.com/sports/jenkins/article/Big-waves-lure-surfers-to-Mavericks
    -competition-5169941.php.

23 Andrew Cave, "Twitter Cofounder Biz Stone's Seven Secrets For Starting And Leading A
    Successful Business," *Forbes*, June 18, 2014, www.forbes.com/sites/andrewcave/2014/06/18
    /twitter-co-founder-biz-stones-seven-secrets-for-starting-and-leading-a-successful-business/.

CHAPTER 9: NEVER SURF ALONE

1   "Unconventional Wisdom: Nathan Fletcher," *Surfer*, September 15, 2015, www
    .surfermag.com/features/unconventional-wisdom-nathan-fletcher/#QxX4
    RH21reMZxY6W.97.

2   Matt Warshaw, *Maverick's: The Story of Big-Wave Surfing* (San Francisco: Chronicle Books,
    2000), 89.

3   Ibid.

4   Ibid., 88.

5   Ibid., 90.

6   "Who Owns This Wave? No One," posted by Mavericks Surf Company, December 23, 2012,
    www.jeffclarkmavericks.com/jeff-clark-blog/2012/12/23/who-owns-this-wave/.

7   Ibid.

8   "Riding Giants—Laird Hamilton Surfing Teahupoo," YouTube video, posted by Jeff
    Robinson, November 29, 2009, https://www.youtube.com/watch?v=xF5tWOcc6Is.

9   "Listen in Full: Bruce Irons Interview," *Surfing* Magazine, August 3, 2015, www
    .surfingmagazine.com/blogs/listen-in-full-bruce-irons-interview/.

10 Ibid.

11 "Matt Meola's Spindle 540 (and Home)," *Surfing* Magazine, May 16, 2015, www.surfing
    magazine.com/video/matt-meolas-spindle-540/#kL5VeVq5HvFwUQ8W.97.

12 Ibid.

NOTES

13   Ben Mondy, "7 Best Excuses Not to Surf Big Waves," GrindTV, March 18, 2015, www
.grindtv.com/travel/7-best-excuses-not-to-surf-big-waves/#3R7hh1ZLvRxvmWik.99.

14   "Surfline's Big Wave Roundtable 2012—Uncut," YouTube video, posted by *Surfline*, September 15, 2014, www.youtube.com/watch?v=RCunB1DG9as.

15   Matt Warshaw, Maverick's: The Story of Big-Wave Surfing (San Francisco: Chronicle Books, 2000), 98.

16   Maya Gabeira to Shaun Tomson, personal email, November 10, 2013.

17   "Ocean Bombs Land in the Nazaré Lineup," Surfertoday.com, November 30, 2014, www
.surfertoday.com/surfing/11216-ocean-bombs-land-in-the-nazare-lineup.

18   Ibid.

19   Nic Lamb interview, August 20, 2015, Santa Monica, CA.

20   Alex Wade, "Tom Curren: Surfer Immortal," Huck, March 23, 2008, www
.huckmagazine.com/ride/surf/tom-curren/

21   Stephanie Gilmore, "Style According to Steph," *Surfer*, November 26, 2015, www
.surfermag.com/features/style-according-to-stephanie-gilmore/#DQtl7wB6T
IJemaZb.99.

22   Caitlin Fitzsimmons, "3D-Printed Surfboard Maker 'Disrupt Surfing' Rides Wave of Interest in Asia," *Business Review Weekly*, April 28, 2015, www.brw.com.au/p/entrepreneurs/printed
_surfboard_maker_disrupt_UfwHdYAaNWfAZweU4aS7CM.

CHAPTER 10: STAY STOKED!

1   Joel Tudor, "Hooked," *Surfer*, July 16, 2015, www.surfermag.com/photos
/hooked/#c2f041cd2a#tLRierh0041YVbLD.97.

2   Dorian Paskowitz, PhD, "Unconventional Wisdom," as told to Kimball Taylor in 2010,
Surfer, November 12, 2014, www.surfermag.com/features/unconventional
-wisdom-doc-paskowitz/#vh8MIEgt5MGwZlgY.97.

3   Ibid.

4   Shaun Tomson and Patrick Moser, *Surfer's Code* (Salt Lake City: Gibbs Smith, 2006).

5   Ibid.

6   Jeff Clark, "A Short History," posted by Mavericks Surf Company, accessed January 2015,
www.jeffclarkmavericks.com/about-jeff-clark/history/.

7   "Surfline's Big Wave Roundtable 2012—Uncut," YouTube video, posted by Surfline,
September 15, 2014, www.youtube.com/watch?v=RCunB1DG9as.

8   Nico Guilis, "Secrets of the Ultimate Surfer Girl," Harper's Bazaar, April 7, 2015, www
.harpersbazaar.com/culture/features/a10504/secrets-of-the-ultimate-surfer-girl/.

9   "I'm Keala Kennelly and I'm a Surfer: Keala Kennelly at TEDxMalibu," YouTube video,
posted by TEDx Talks, February 2, 2014, www.youtube.com/watch?v=eSvsrzPCZ5o.

10   Ibid.

11   "About Mark Healy," accessed January 2016, www.markhealeywaterman.com/about/.

12   Ben Martin, "Why Surfers Make Great Entrepreneurs (And Vice Versa)," March 21, 2014.
www.blog.up.co/2014/03/21/surfers-make-great-entrepreneurs-vice-versa/.

13   "Happy Birthday, Andy Irons," *Surfing*, July 23, 2015, www.surfingmagazine.com/video
/happy-birthday-andy-irons/.

14   Ibid.

15   Robert Pursell, "How the Silicon Beach Surfers Club Does Business Between Sets," GrindTV, June 17, 2015, www.grindtv.com/surf/how-the-silicon-beach-surfers -club-does-business-between-sets/#hOeioBrdagETsSIx.97.

16   Ibid.

17   Ibid.

18   Ibid.

19   "Star Quarterback Balks at No-Surfing Clause," Surfline, July 1, 2015, www.surfline.com/ surf-news/first-round-draft-pick-marcus-mariota-says-maybe-not-to-20 -million-dollar-contract-with-tennessee-titans-star-_129037/.

20   Shaun Tomson, "#1 Kelly Slater: Surfer Celebrates the 50 Greatest Surfers of All Time," Surfer, July 22, 2010, www.surfermag.com/features/number_1_kelly_slater /#XsUD23VefEvVg8Bw.99.

21   Ibid.

22   Ibid.

23   Ibid.

24   Kelly Slater, "Hooked," Surfer, July 16, 2015, www.surfermag.com/photos /hooked/#603d378956.

25   Dale Webster, "Hooked," Surfer, July 16, 2015, www.surfermag.com/photos /hooked/#6e41a422d4.

26   Herbie Fletcher, "Hooked," Surfer, July 16, 2015, www.surfermag.com /photos/hooked/#be092536be.

27   Ben Martin, "Why Surfers Make Great Entrepreneurs (And Vice Versa)," March 21, 2014, blog.up.co/2014/03/21/surfers-make-great-entrepreneurs-vice-versa/.

EPILOGUE

1   Ellen Wright, "'Super Sessions' Follows Women Big Wave Surfing," GrindTV video, December 1, 2015, www.grindtv.com/surf/super-sessions-follows -women-big-wave-surfing/#dkv3t9MYQb9AwjRf.99.

2   "Surfing Included in the Tokyo 2020 Olympic Games," Surfertoday.com, September 28, 2015, www.surfertoday.com/surfing/12213-surfing-included-in-the -tokyo-2020-olympic-games.

NOTES

INDEX

INDEX

179